NO MORE

By Lizbeth & Meath Byrne

This is a biography of a mother and daughter's life, experienced together. From a very different perspective.

A story from both sides of addiction. The addict and the affected family member.

Please set aside the things you think you know about addiction for an open mind about this book. We hope you may see similarities, not differences. Addiction can be displayed in different forms with many different substances.

Meath; I dedicate this book in gratitude to all the amazing people in the fellowships who have helped me over the years.

To the newcomers, the sponsees, sponsors and addicts still fighting, you help me more than you might ever know...

To Lizbeth for your incredible love and support, words don't ever seem to do justice to how proud I am that you are my Ma.

To Source, for your eternal loving guidance, without whom none of this would be...

And to my new spiritual healing family. May we bring healing, hope and faith to whomever may need it. Thank you for taking me to the next dimension! Ohana.

Lizbeth dedicates this book to all those who have suffered and relate to this trauma.

To Meath, my love, my inspiration, my learning through this roller coaster life, my deepest gratitude.

The proceeds from this book are going to the Lizbeth & Meath Byrne Addiction Foundation and to a non-profit spiritual healing centre.

Contents

1. Meath asks for help

I rang my ma.

Things must have been bad at the end to believe it myself and admit that I needed help finally. And honestly.

I don't remember what was said but I told her I was going to rehab.

I had rung a help line on the Internet who put me through to a rehab. They said they had a place for me next week. I knew by then I wouldn't be in the same frame of mind, let alone still here.

"No, please you have to come and pick me up now!" I pleaded in my usual way. Thankfully they agreed and told me they'd send someone in the morning.

I remember fearfully thinking 'I need new clothes!' Of all the things to worry about, my image was right up there, even though I was dying inside.

As long as I looked a certain way, I could create an image of what I wanted people to think of me, helping me be accepted.

Yes, they said bring some comfy clothes.

I went out onto the street. It became like my next adventure, getting well. A spark of hope inside me. My life in the past few years had been one dramatic disaster after another.

I only got half way down the road when I couldn't walk any further. I sat in a doorstep and noticed the world had turned grey, I didn't have much strength to get up.

I felt so disconnected from life, I was looking at people walking by and I didn't feel like I belonged in their world.

I felt alien, listless, hopeless and cut off.

I rested for a bit and then carried on to a market stall and bought some socks. I quickly retreated home, all of my energy depleted.

That night I threw all the last of my stash down the toilet.

Ten minutes later, a feeling of doom came over me... what a stupid thing to do! I can't make it through the night. I need more!

Fear engulfed me.

I didn't know anything then about being an addict, how it was totally out of my control what was happening. A puppet on a string, slave to drugs and drink and I had no idea that there was another way to live without my crutches.

I wasn't going to rehab wanting to stop, I just wanted to know how to live like a 'normal' person and recreationally use drugs and alcohol.

Like friends I knew that had a 9-5 job and partied at the weekends.

I couldn't do that.

I had a 24/7, 365 addiction. It never stopped and it hardly slept.

Somehow I made it through the night, I must have drunk my carton wine.

The next morning I dragged my worn-out pink suitcase down the stairs and left the hovel of a room I had been staying in.

I got into the car they sent to begin the journey to rehab.

I remember the driver, a large smiling ginger-haired man, full of stories of people he'd picked up and taken to the Centre.

He told me about the ones who would arrive with drugs on them.

All I could think was those lucky f&£@s! Why didn't I think of that, why wasn't I going to rehab high!

Failed again.

I was always a failure. Or a superstar... There wasn't much middle ground in my thinking.

I'd always tried to do well, always wanted to not do what I was doing, to not let people down as I often did with missed appointments, promises, trips home. Or to not get too out of my head each time.

I had the best intentions. But 90% of the time they did not go to plan.

Addiction showed up time and again to ruin the day.

I arrived at the treatment centre. It was huge, which I liked, there should be lots of places to get lost in.

I was staying in the Boat House, the more solitary part of the centre, there was a communal residency close by but I chose to hide myself away.

There were daily group meetings I didn't want to attend.

I just wanted to eat what I wanted which because I wasn't taking drugs, had immediately switched back to starvation mode. An eating disorder I had before I started using re-emerged.

Controlling what I ate, not eating enough, just strange snacks on my own at night, small binges followed by guilt and shame and more restriction - another form of using I later found out.

The only thing I would do was the private one to one meeting with my designated therapist.

As soon as he saw me he told me I was a love addict as well.

He brought out a book and told me to read about myself!

I thought he was an absolute fool who knew nothing about me. I was just a drug addict, but to be honest, he could see right through me. He told me I was selfish and a manipulator, that I'd manipulated everyone. That I was a victim and I'd played the victim my whole life. He was right. But I did not realise that for a good few years to come.

I made a few friends, similar to me, we laughed together, sharing crazy using stories from the past that bonded us – things most people would find horrifying were our in-jokes.

Three weeks in and things were going well, too well really, because we were all going to have, can you believe it, a dinner party.

One guy had access to a kitchen.

Wow, I thought I'm actually making some friends here some sober ones, which I've never done.

That afternoon a new kid turned up and we all got together playing pool that evening. He started talking about my drug of choice. Or how I like to put it now is my drug of absolutely no choice. We each had one, whether it be pills or coke or booze. The one that gets under your skin that you can't have enough of. The saviour, the daydream.

He went on and on talking about it, how he took it etc. No one else was doing that drug, they had other addictions. It set off a fire inside me.

He said he'd be able to get it into rehab for me if I wanted. He was only a young boy really and whatever his motive, it worked.

The fire was lit inside me and my mind became completely obsessed. I really did not know what I was going to do. The boy had lied and could get nothing.

But I had to use.

There was no two ways about it.

I've learned now about powerlessness over drugs. Powerlessness over my mind. I had no power over my mind at that time to do anything about it.

My friend was going to a doctor's appointment the next day in a taxi. He had been in the rehab a long time and had privileges. With his agreement, the next morning I hid in a bush and jumped in his taxi when he was half way down the drive.

I had a bit of money and a credit card in my pocket and went to where I knew I could pick up and had my first relapse.

I got enough to normally last a weekend but finished it all that night. The following morning I got more of the same and was done with that by that night. A monster. No care, no thoughts, just more!

I was banished from the rehab.

They were shocked which in truth shocked me. An addict had used again! All the patients were angry with me! I wasn't welcome! What!

That's what addicts do, they use, that's why they are called addicts. They use even when they really don't want to.

I'm not just in there for breaking a champagne glass, I really wanted help, I just had no tools to help my mental state.

I remember Ma telling me I had to come home, I knew I couldn't get my drug there. Anguish. Doom. Fear.

I asked for help. There was no one there but I prayed someone was listening. I felt hopeless again and in the same old position. How was I ever going to stop or get a hold of things? It seemed impossible and the need was so strong.

I wasn't religious but had been brought up praying by my bed at night with Ma, to bless our friends and family and to give thanks for what we have. I turned my back on it later on – you would do, having a life like mine.

I asked again, please, God, help me. Someone help me!

Meath; Finding my feet. Feeling alone, scared… but grounded and hopeful, connecting with life again. Photo taken after two weeks rehab, the first few weeks without drugs and alcohol in years.

2. Meath. The Phone Call

"Hello, Ma." Her voice was soft. She didn't often ring me out of the blue.

I was usually ringing her mobile, desperate for her to answer, not knowing where she was. In Dublin somewhere.

"Ma, I have a problem!" Panic rushed through my head, which problem now.

"You know, don't you?" Which one? I thought. I waited for her to continue, held my breath, not daring to speak. Impending doom thoughts in my always troubled mind.

"I've checked into a rehab."

Silenced shock. I didn't know where to begin. Dozens of questions buzzed round in my head. No, she's not an addict, what of? Visions raced into my head, needles hanging out of her arm, falling over, dirty, living on the streets, bottle of empty gin in her hand, in the company of other addicts... My mind shut down. I felt an unknown nervous feeling.

Was she really an addict? I took a deep breath and I tried to clear my thoughts and think of my pretty girl, my beautiful daughter who could be so kind, so loving... so volatile.

My eyes filled.

"I'm going tomorrow morning," Meath continued.

I felt terror and relief. In spite of all the crazy years, I knew I trusted my daughter. It must be bad. I just didn't want to see the reality. But here it was.

I tried to breathe properly. "You know I'll support you all the way, just let me know what you need me to do," was my plaintive answer.

Instinctively I calmed my voice. Perhaps from lack of air of this unknown crisis.

7

She obviously knew what she was doing. She had reached her bottom pit. Thank God, thank whoever, this was an opening for help.

At last.

One question at a time, when, where... How had she found this rehab, was it a good one, but what did I know anyway?

"I'm going in tomorrow. They are sending a car and they need you to ring tomorrow with a credit card," Meath continued.

"Yes, of course," I stuttered. It almost sounded like she was checking into a hotel. I was in a shocked dream.

And there started our new journey.

I lived in France, in the mid-south countryside, Meath in Dublin.

Meath asked me to come over as soon as I could, of course, and I wanted to know what was going on for €5,000 for a few weeks. The price shook me but if it's her life, our lifeline.

Then she'd be cured, right!   It would be well worthwhile. I would do whatever it took.

It was no use asking her father for help, he wouldn't understand, let alone give me any money towards this – no one would understand. I didn't.

I would use some of my parents' money they had left me. I got organised and booked a flight to Dublin.

3. Lizbeth's first visit to rehab...

I hopped on the boat. It could take about eight passengers and had a little cabin midships to keep off the sea spray from the choppy waves. As we rounded the coast the building came into view. I saw an ominous dark old building, with turrets. This was the rehab my daughter had found in the middle of nowhere, on a small island. Apparently there was a causeway entrance but only at low tide.

The skipper asked me where my daughter was staying. I said I thought the Boathouse. He smiled.

I hugged my daughter on the pontoon but there was a sort of nervous coolness between us than our usual greetings.

Meath showed me around as if it was a new school. A surreal déjà-vu feeling swept over me. I walked round murmuring inanely at various things. "This is the games room," Meath quipped. I glanced at her. She looked okay. But then I didn't know what an addict looked like. My daughter apparently. Normal, like you and me, chatting away. When she went to boarding school she complained about the teachers, but now it was about the therapists. I'd always had images that drug addicts were people who are frightening-looking.

Basically, I was in shock. Was she in the right place? This was a beautiful, slightly sinister, old building, with old oak floors, high ceilings, comfortable sofas. Shabby chic I think they call it nowadays. The dreamy nightmare continued.

Meath introduced to me to several people. "This is an inmate, or that was a helper. This is a therapist. This is the kitchen where I'm not allowed yet," she murmured.

The first therapist we had an appointment with was extraordinary, sort of a balding boffin, with huge books piled up in front of him. Very intense. He said weird things and I assumed he wasn't really talking about my daughter. He was insinuating this would take a long time. Surely they would explain to Meath what was the matter, give her advice, medicine and send her home, well again.

I left in a daze, numb. Meath gave many promises, she now wanted to be clean. A different meaning of the word.

Somehow, I didn't feel confident of anything but then I was completely out of my depth. This was a new world, a new way of life, a different language.

I left my daughter at this place, feeling very lost and alone.

Going through life's motions on automatic but somehow apart.

I landed back in France. My dogs greeted me, I sat on the terrace with their wagging tails.

I wept.

When my marriage collapsed about fifteen years ago, most of my close family had departed this world. I couldn't live in a small town in Southern Ireland anymore. I needed a complete new way of life. We – Meath and I – moved 'home' to the mid-south of France in the countryside. Meath lived in Dublin and commuted home for college holidays and many visits. We were very close, but I hadn't been able to tackle her problem. Not really sure what it was and always thinking and hoping it was a youthful stage which would pass soon and she would grow out of it.

I escaped to the fields with my dogs, fresh air, long walking, trying to free my confused brain and be positive.

Meath was on her way to health, after all it was her who'd made this great decision. I was proud of her.

Just maybe I'd get my lovely child back from this constant worry.

There was hope, something I hadn't had since the slow but steady chaotic years which started when Meath was about twelve years old.

At first, I thought it was just a hormonal stage, making my daughter into an occasional monster. My mother said it was a 'phase' and reassured me she would grow out of it.

But after changing schools four times in three years, crazy parties, passionate teenage romances with lovesick boyfriends constantly ringing or calling round and lots of arguments as most mothers and daughters have, I wasn't so sure anything would ever change.

I lived a life being in a sort of shocked state, lurching from one crisis into another. Surely, I hadn't been this crazy.

What drama next? Where would I be rescuing her from next?

What and how much would the bill be, from anywhere in the world.

How many headmasters had I pleaded with to please give her a chance after she had been expelled from one school after only five weeks. Another, she refused to get out of the car. I physically dragged her out. She ran away the next day.

After going from one school to another I found one who put her on a sort of probation for the first few terms.

In a way I hadn't really been too surprised at my daughter, really, raging hormones, angry with the world for no reason, seeming to hate nearly everyone in it, sometimes herself.

I am a mother from the liberal sixties, who went slightly mad with marijuana, free love and music. I thought the best way was to be an understanding, patient mother. I would try and stay her friend, get to know her friends, invite them to our house, somehow be in her life. It would all get better.

I'd wonder which school should she have gone to, should her father have been in her life more. Beating myself up with the shoulds and should nots.

Her father was 'distant' from us both, even when he was in the house.

It would now get better I reassured myself.

Now, about ten years later, she hadn't grown out of the madness. It was just worse. She was so thin, didn't eat a meal in front of others, squirrelled away snacks and ate at night, watching tv until dawn. Sometimes seeming frightened of sleeping on her own, she'd come into my room and listen to music or a film on her laptop with her earphones in.

For some of the time she would be the lovely, loving girl I knew she really was inside.

Sometimes I would listen to her on her mobile late at night chatting to her city friends, unbeknownst to me drinking all the alcohol she could find, putting the empty bottles back in the cupboard. I suppose she thought I wouldn't notice. Well, I didn't until days after she left.

I didn't want to believe she could drink that amount on her own. I would kid myself that maybe there wasn't much left in the bottles anyway.

It would all be better when she passed her exams and started working. I continually tried to believe the next phase, the next year she would be passionate about something other than living this mindless life.

She never seemed to be able to finish her exams on time, starting work projects but not continuing with anything for long. Always promising me she would.

Her clothes loose, her hands shaking.

Of course, I had tried to take her to various counsellors through the years. Once we sat on a psychiatrist's sofa and Meath wouldn't even say one word. One school offered counselling, Meath couldn't concentrate on her work, they said. She was an intelligent girl, just about made it through her exams. She seemed to have ambition, but not the effort or concentration to be able to achieve or finish anything.

Any available funds she could acquire from her father or I seemed to vanish quickly.

When she went to the City for college. I paid her rent and food as far as I could. My motherly instinct would fill her empty fridge when I visited her. I encouraged, bullied, persuaded her to go to college, talked to her teachers and was in her life without being too interfering! I gave very little cash, trying to find balance.

Meath loved trying to shock me, her friends, schools. Her world was her personal rebellion place. She said one day, "You had your rebellion in the sixties. We have nothing to push against, you've all done it, free love, music, drugs."

Whatever I did I always felt I either hadn't done enough, or maybe too much. Constant exasperation and not understanding.

Asking myself what and if I was doing something wrong. Should I get out of her life, sort of let her go and see what would happen? I so wanted her to pass exams, thinking that would help her feel better in herself and ambition would follow.

When Meath came home to France we would have happy relaxed friendly times, she would promise to work and study. I tried to believe in her.

She would surely find a worthwhile career, a passion and feel good about herself, then progress.

I was in cuckoo land.

4. Lizbeth. More surprises

Meath rang to say whether I could arrange for her suitcase to be collected as she had left the rehab saying it was no good!

Now what?

I rang the secretary in a panic, who filled me in on their side and told me Meath had brought drugs into the rehab so they would not allow her to return.

Expelled again.

In the meantime, where was she? I felt panic rising, back in my state of fright and fear.

I rang her mobile, she didn't answer...

Again... It was all happening again... I felt ill. I knew now where the phrase 'worried sick' came from. Where was she? What was she doing?

A few hours later she finally answered. Giving me her usual excuses and saying the rehab was useless. She talked of another rehab in England, whether I would look up this one or that one had been recommended by someone! It seemed like I was looking for schools again.

Trying to find a rehab in France.

At first I rang a few rehabs in England who instantly wanted a £5,000 credit card payment, non-refundable, before they would go and collect my daughter. I was exhausted and felt far away.

I wanted her home nearer me. Mother's instincts told me I could make her better. I couldn't keep paying these exorbitant amounts if she wasn't going to, at least, stay for the cure.

I started looking on the Internet, not believing any respectable rehab would be advertising there (this was many years ago now).

"La Bonne Route" popped up on the screen. The only one within about an hour from our home. A little hope. Would they speak English?

I felt desperate, maybe this was my answer. I rang. A calm voice answered, yes in English and yes, Meath could join their programme. There was a room and I could visit tomorrow. I rang to let Meath know.

No answer.

5. Meath. Coming home... but rehab home

I remember the day I was going home.

It sounds bizarre, but I felt a force behind me, pushing me forward. I could feel it when I was walking to the airport disbelievingly and thinking I don't want to do this.

I don't want to go home, the addiction was on me again, the switch had been flicked. I didn't want to recover anymore. I didn't want help, I didn't want rehab.

I didn't want to go, but there was something pushing me onwards, I could feel it. I had tears streaming down my face, silent tears that didn't stop rolling.

I thought Ma would collect me from the airport, maybe I'd be able to talk her into a holiday instead.

But I got picked up by a treatment centre. When I saw the man, I just knew he was for me and I knew it was the end and I broke down. The whole way there in the car he went on, "I don't have to take you here. You don't have to come with me, if you don't have a problem?"

I kept saying "Okay, I'll go home."

And him "Okay, if you don't have a problem... but you do, don't you? Tell me about the drugs you take..."

He got out of me how many drugs I'd been doing, how long and my history.

We went round and round whether I needed to go, whether I had a problem on and on.

By that time we had arrived. It was a very different place to the last grand escape, a tiny bungalow. As I walked in they gave me a Valium which I appreciated. How do I get them to give me more? My first thought.

The next day, after my second Valium, when their backs were turned, I vaulted the wall, scraping and tearing my jeans and knees. I jumped down into the street below.

I was running, I'd run my whole life, from everything, it was what I knew best. Adrenaline, it made me feel good, alive.

I hated being hemmed in, they took my passport away as well and told me I had to stay three months!

I knew the area and where I could get certain drugs and drink, but I just wanted that one drug and I was too tired to mess about.

I felt broken and desperate.

I borrowed a phone at a petrol station. What a sight I must have looked. I used to shake uncontrollably after a few hours without drinking and using. I would ring my hands together and chew on my cheeks and clench my jaw.

I rang Ma. It rang and rang.

I got the answerphone. "Come pick me up. Get me out of here, I'm fine. I'll do anything, just get me out. I hate it. I'll get better, I just need a break," I shouted and pleaded.

I could manipulate Ma, give her promises – empty promises I see now but which I honestly believed I could keep. I didn't actively think, Oh, I'm manipulating my Ma. I was terrified. Not of the rehab but of myself, of my addiction and of the terrible monster inside me that needed drugs and unconsciousness.

I fooled myself and I fooled everyone else all those years.

I was completely deluded.

Every way out was closed for me and the rehab came to get me.

I do believe I had to be cut off by my family in order to get better. The more Ma threw money at me or helped me out, paid my bills and put me up, the more it enabled me to carry on the way I was. Burying our heads in the sand.

There weren't many options left. However strong my addiction was, I wasn't going to prostitute myself.

I had no fight left.

I went back and stayed the three months, with a warning if I ran again they would have me sectioned and locked up. I did the therapy. I tried.

There were only a few people and we got introduced to 12-step recovery, to Cocaine Anonymous, Alcoholics Anonymous, Narcotics Anonymous, Co-dependency Anonymous and Overeaters Anonymous!

I went to a meeting every day for three months and made some friends. People that cared for seemingly no reason, people just like me, with stories like mine. Some of them were old and a little boring, but I could understand them and I respected them.

The bad times seemed to bring us together.

I had been to many psychiatrists, therapists, hypnotists, you name it, but none of them had ever touched me like this. All the antidepressants, anti-anxiety pills, they didn't work for me. They just muddied the situation, which the dark addict part of me liked, but left me still with this hole inside that needed to be ´fixed.´

The problem was I knew I would use again. The thought of using again after my time got me through the long painful days. Obsessing about my drug.

6. Lizbeth's visit to rehab en France

Finally, Meath rang me. I said I'd found a rehab near home. I'd like her here. Amazingly, she agreed. I hadn't told her I hadn't seen it. I picked up my car keys. I'd better go and visit it quickly.

As I went into the old comfortable-looking villa I noted an air of tranquillity.

A lovely soft-spoken lady greeted me. We sat in a small room and I truly can't remember what I said. I remember crying a lot, years of choked up feelings, but she gave me hope and never made me feel anything was wrong.

It didn't feel like a clinic, just a quiet secluded old house.

This lady, Neelam, smiled at my confusion and tears, my hesitant jumbled words.

She instilled a chink of hope and a sense of trust which I needed, after all, I would be leaving my daughter with them. She just seemed to understand.

I asked as I was leaving if Meath could get out easily. Neelam reassured me no one had been able to leave, it was a very secure garden and house.

Relief flooded through me – now to get her here.

We had discussed collecting Meath at the airport that evening. I desperately wanted to see her, hug her, tell her it would all be alright but I knew she would wangle her way out of going into the rehab until the next day. I knew I would be powerless of her often strong determination in arguments.

Neelam suggested it would be much better if I let another therapist collect her. Better for us both.

It was time to leave this to the experts. I was exhausted, mentally and physically. I didn't know which way to turn. This seemed a safer option, plus I didn't really trust myself

not to give in to Meath and allow her home for one night...
Then, more nights. I – we - would be lost again.

Later that evening my mobile started ringing, I could see it
was Meath. She must have landed and seen I wasn't there
at the arrival gate.

About ten unanswered calls later, it stopped. I sat and
watched the phone ring. My heart shattered. I felt I was in
a cocoon of numb emptiness, ignorance and a huge
sadness.

Neelam rang me later, said Meath had arrived and she
was fine.

A little relief.

I poured a strong drink and started smoking, one after
another, sitting in the dusk, wondering.

I proceeded to argue things out in my mind. Yes, I liked
a drink or two most evenings while I cooked, who didn't?
Right now, it helped my nerves. The cigarettes made me
cough and tasted vile, but I ploughed on one after the other
as if it would help.

As the vodka and smoke settled me somehow, I did a
bit more self-reproach.

Too kind, too tolerant, why hadn't I been braver and
yanked her off to rehab earlier when I had seen her
shaking, her clothes looking like they were one size too
big, or was that the fashion?

It wasn't all bad, she'd had a good upbringing, happy,
lots of pals, an open sharing friendship with me. Until the
addiction galloped away from us.

7. Lizbeth escapes to the mountains

The next morning after Meath's arrival, I drove with my dogs into the mountains. We walked for about two to three hours.

Peace and countryside seemed to always help me recover my sanity.

I felt hope again, but kept it in a controlled place. Just in case of future surprises.

On the drive back down from the hills, my mobile started pinging with lots of incoming messages. I had obviously been in an area with no signal.

I pulled over and saw all these missed calls arriving from an unknown number.

I started listening to the voice messages.

Meath had escaped over a wall, borrowed some unfortunate man's mobile, what a frantic desperate state she must have been in.

Message one: "Come and get me, I can't take it." Angry voice.

Message two: "Please come and get me." Still cross.

Message three: "Please, please, Ma, come and get me. I can't take it, I'll be good." Pleading and desperate.

A few messages later: "Oh, okay, I'll do it."

Last message: "OK, I'll go back." Accepted cross voice.

Amazing how fate intervened. No doubt, if I hadn't been out of phone coverage I would have rescued her, hugs and tears, then despair again. I really wasn't strong enough for this. Was I a bad parent? Too loving?

I carried on with my personal inner argument. Had I been too loving? Too giving? But then, if Meath pushed me too far I could get very cross with her. I tried to have a harmonious life with my daughter, especially now she was in her twenties. I just didn't understand all this addiction thing.

I wanted to cry, scream, wail, but to whom...

I returned home and rang Neelam to tell her about my messages and where someone could go and pick her up. I'd decided not to rub in their embarrassment regarding the wall, we had enough of a problem. They apologised profusely and said it had never happened before. I knew my daughter's determination and mental strength. Imagine how desperate and cunning one could be, to escape, needing your drug so much.

In the back of my mind, it was almost laughable.

There was now silence for a week. No mobile. This was difficult, what were they doing to her. It was like boarding school prison camp.

The first Sunday afternoon, I could visit. I was nervous, she introduced me to a few friends, other inmates then we went and sat outside in the garden. Meath puffed on one cigarette after another. "They allow us to smoke. They can't take all the addictions away at once," she told me. I mentioned I'd started again. It was an awkward visit, neither of us really knowing what to say or what either had been going through during that week. Like two strangers who knew each other very well, but each in their own world of pain.

I left feeling isolated and adrift in our future.

These next few weeks passed in a similar fashion, visiting Sunday afternoons for an upsetting and disorientated few hours.

8. Meath's thoughts in rehab

I believe it couldn't ever have worked for me to stay clean for good in the second rehab, as I felt I had been 'forced' into it, shut out of home, collected by a therapist, passport taken away, mobile taken away, no contact with the outside world. I felt very angry.

I rebelled about being locked in there and the defiance in me was strong.

I likened it to being at boarding school.

I had never wanted school. It had always been such a battle to go.

I don't think it's the same for all addicts, some are high achievers.

I wanted to achieve greatness and had huge dreams but I just couldn't get it together, living in fantasy land and dipping in and out of fear of failure and criticism. I just couldn't get my mind in gear to do anything but gear! And when I was young, I buried myself in books and wild imagination.

Even when I worked hard, I was never good enough for the toughest judge of all. Me. Needing a crutch to feel alright or to perform better.

Something that has taken me nine years to get near to accepting and even understanding is that perfection is not achievable for an addict and I will make myself ill trying to make it so.

Nothing will ever be good enough and that is the nature of the disease of addiction.

The hole in the soul.

Another addiction trait is hating being told what to do, so being in this rehab was like being trapped. I didn't believe they could help or that I could learn anything and I was going to show them anyway!

I believe if you personally don't want it then I don't think you can have it! Not for long, anyway.

It can't be drummed into you by psychiatrists, doctors, parents... anyone.

You can go to meetings or keep going in and out of rehab, but if you don't really want it, you won't get it without divine intervention or without having some sort of spiritual awakening. By that I mean, clear thinking of belief in the truth. The real truth.

Which is... Whoa, hang on a minute.... maybe I really am an addict, maybe I can't stop doing whatever it is I'm doing. And stop fighting against the world the whole time.

Like being in delusion or denial or both continually.

I felt I went in and out of both regularly.

They told me I had to write down my life story. I believe it's meant to wake you up to what the hell has been going on in your life, to see it in the cold light of day and admit to yourself your powerlessness over your addiction and see the unmanageability of it. To acknowledge your life doesn't function anymore or is seriously lacking balance and that you keep doing the same harmful thing over and over, hoping for a different outcome.

My first life story was part ego trip, part drama queen... it was for show! I cringingly remember telling another addict in the first centre it was my life story reading today, so she would come along… I sat in front of a big room and took my place as victim, hero, junkie ´the worst, best addict of them all!´ Shudder. Cringe.

I didn't get serious until the second rehab, when I spilled my guts with truth and despair. I didn't need to make it worse, it was already a train wreck.

What I learned in those first few weeks is that the illness of addiction has three parts which qualifies you to be 'a real deal addict' – not just someone who gets addicted to an addictive substance, gets clean from it and doesn't do it again.

I mean someone who goes back time and again to the detriment of themselves. AKA hopeless addict.

These types suffer with:
An Obsessive mind;
A physical allergy for more; and
A spiritual malady.

I began to try and make friends with my addict, to step back from the damaging negative thoughts and choose another way. I learned a new voice. I had to re-wire my brain.

I learned the disease centres in the mind, which makes a lot of sense as to why the afflicted person repeats the same damaging behaviour, even after they have had a spell of abstinence.

It's a mental problem.

That's why I do the same stupid thing over and over again, expecting a different result; because my mind is sick, it tells me there's nothing wrong with me.

It is the only disease that tells you you don't have it.

Maddening!

So that's when you know you are dealing with an addict, when they really want to get well, desperately, but they just can't get it together. Or they want to do the work but can't as they get side-tracked by negative thinking and damaging behaviour.

A lot of us also don't believe they are an addict and yet they use every day, wrecking their lives and others'.

It's very confusing for the addict and for the affected family.

It's also really hard for the addict to stay well especially in the beginning, because the disease is so strong - if you have something that's always telling you you don't have it, that you're okay – you believe it. You have to fight your mind the whole time.

Or maybe it tells you you're so bad you're beyond help and there's no possible way you could ever change. It's so strong.

When I was first in treatment, I would look at people in meetings and think I was above them or below them but never part of them and I honestly didn't believe that I suffered with some of the things they spoke of and I didn't want to!

People talked about obsessive minds and I'd think, you poor people I couldn't connect with it, I had no self-awareness.

This mind was all I'd ever known and the last few years being near constantly sedated I couldn't identify who or what I really was or felt.

I didn't know that your mind might possibly not need to tell you a million things all day long and drive you crazy doing damaging things and how using took all that away for me and brought me "peace" whilst it worked in a very false sense.

After my first couple of meetings I found it easy to blend in. I felt accepted for the first time, although I'm not sure I wanted to be. In fact, I really didn't want to be there. I wanted to be back with my friends getting high and having a laugh, but that ship had sailed... for now, anyway.

I'm Meath and I'm an addict, alcoholic, anorexic, love addict, co-dependent, sex addict! Whatever relevant for the meeting that day. Lol.

It's your admission, your name and affliction.

I owned being an addict. My badges shone brightly through my bloodshot eyes and shaking fists that I used to sit on, clinging to the bottom of the chair rattling from the double espressos I had necked before going in.

My scars showed; real as well as metaphorical but I hid my co-dependency and eating disorder in shame, they didn't seem as glamorous to me as a filthy drug habit!

Each person spoke, if they wanted, about whatever was going on for them. There is a brutal honesty about it all and genuine loving care, which strips down the masks that we wear outside to fit in.

You don't talk about whatever anyone else has said, which gives you a feeling of freedom in what you are saying.

No one to answer to, just acceptance and a validation of your feelings.

You share for yourself and to help others.

In rehab it's different, you talk about yourself and all your problems, and others get to have their say about what you share, which definitely sparked some animosity between a few that I saw!

I found I didn't mind the talking in La Bonne Route, especially as there were only three of us most of the time.

I learned a lot and was taken to meetings outside the clinic which was my favourite part of the day. Escape. Even if it was to an old town hall's back room. It was nice to be out and meet new people... and smoke!

I could identify with other addicts and alcoholics, especially the feelings when they were children before they ever started using. The loneliness you feel inside, even when there are people with you. The feeling that you aren't good enough and the awkwardness of not fitting in.

The whole illness I learned is self; self-inflating, as well as destructing. Self-obsession. It took me a long time to understand that as well, as I thought I was kind and sweet, which I was but I also spent most of the day thinking about me, of what people thought of me, what I had done wrong or well... What I looked like. What this piece of bread would do to my thighs... Where was the next fix? What I had said in detail about whatever subject to whatever random person... on and on.

I couldn't see my actions were affecting the whole family. I just thought it's all on me, my hardship, my pain, my drug problem, my mind. And if you had a mind like mine, you'd be driven to all this depression and darkness too and you would have to take drink or drugs – this I learned is the spiritual malady.

The hole in my soul!

So I sat around talking in the meetings at the rehab. I talked and I smoked and I complained!

I could wallow in my melancholy like I had done for years.

When the guest speakers came they would talk about how wonderful their lives were now in recovery... Those are the ones I absolutely hated!

I would dive under the duvet and pretend I was ill when those happy flappy people came in. I didn't want to hear it. It sounded alien and boring the way they lived! I just couldn't fathom or identify at all at that point how I would enjoy a sober moment at peace with the world.

They spoke of the beauty in the present, of a sunset, driving slowly down a hill and appreciating life. I just didn't get it!

But I hadn't woken up yet. I was still asleep.

I didn't have the desperation of a month past and the disease had had enough time to be reawakened. My head was telling me things weren't that bad as I hadn't picked up for three weeks.

Things could look rosy pretty quickly.

My mind told me there can't be anything wrong. I'm fine.

The obsessive mind, the denial, the liar in my head – my addict, would make up all kinds of lies that I wasn't really an addict and it was all about my father, my past, my education.

Maybe I was drinking the wrong wine, taking the wrong drug.

Any excuse in the book. I thought I shouldn't take meth next time, I would take cocaine. Not drink vodka. I'd drink whiskey. Maybe I could just smoke pot, my reasoning was madness.

The addiction was thinking for me and I was a victim to its needs.

I was sitting there not realising what was going on and sometimes it can still happen now. Nine years clean but in a different way. If I don't go to meetings for a while my peace of mind goes. My brain says I didn't go last week and I'm okay now, I've things to do, then suddenly I'm snapping at my husband and short with my kids and everyone's the enemy.

If they would just leave me alone and agree with me and do exactly what I need them to then all will be well.

And then I'm back in the madness again! Self, self, self, it's all about me, me, me!

In the beginning I would have used almost immediately if I hadn't gone to a meeting, whereas now I go into negative thinking.

The disease always wants to isolate you.

It tells you that you don't have it. All it wants is for you to be alone, so eventually you can be broken in the dark where things are so bad because you have pushed everyone away. So there is absolutely no other option apart from to use, drink or kill yourself, and that is the bottom line, for me.

We learn in the meetings that "no human power can relieve our alcoholism or addiction".

So my husband can't, my ma can't, and I can't.

I have to want it for me. It was my asking the silent walls of my room, the stars... It's not religious, but my asking a Higher Power and giving up the self 'will' got me well.

I can't do it myself, my will doesn't take me anywhere but backwards. It gets me to a bar, drunk. It gets me scoring drugs. It gets me talking to the wrong type of boys.

I have to give up that self-will. It doesn't mean that I just do nothing. It means I pray to the goodness of the world to help me. I know it sounds mad but it works. Believe me. I was beyond help. Self-defiant to the last and having tried so many different avenues to wellness.

It's strange when you pray. I find it easy as I was brought up praying but I know there are negative things with religions and many people have bad impressions on what 'religious humans' have done wrong in their lives which is understandable, but it's not about us controlling humans, it's about that which created all. The invisible vibration that connects us. The thing that makes electricity work! The energy that created the big bang. The strange feeling you have that something isn't right. Intuition. Goodness, love, nature, a snowflake.

I don't see myself as religious. But I got brought up saying prayers by my bedside with Ma and it was a beautiful experience. I never didn't think there wasn't a God. I didn't question it.

My experience was always nice. We didn't go to church all the time but when we did it was peaceful and everyone was friendly.

I disregarded the negative fire pits of hell talk as it didn't resonate with me. I believed man made that up to gain control over people. My God wanted love, happiness and forgiveness, even then.

Something in me just believed and I see that was a blessing in early recovery as I have witnessed other people who won't believe and they can't seem to find happiness or sobriety for any length of time.

I've met a lot of different people from a lot of different religions and I, with my little knowledge, believe it's not about religion.

It's about believing in a Higher Power as I see it.

Acknowledging there is a power – in this universe, and it's bigger that me.

Go down to the sea, step outside, see the wind blowing a leaf across a field. See the sea crashing against the beach... and if you can't see there's an energy or power bigger that you, then you really need help!

Whether it be scientific or natural or supernatural even, there is a power and it's bigger than you and it can help you.

It doesn't discriminate. It loves you, I'm certain of it.

So, for me in the beginning, I used to pray to the stars as there was a tiny square of window in the rehab where people used to smoke. I used to look up from the four oppressive walls and gaze at the sky and awesome stars and pray – help me, stars. That was all that was needed.

My God is not human, nor male or female, it's a loving energy.

I've felt it. I don't know it, but I feel it and I get great direction from it now I have learned how.

I wrote a story about what God means to me and what I need God to be to me.

God loves and cares about me. He works for me and I work for Him. I need God to forgive me because I've done things that I am ashamed of or that have been harmful to others, things that some religions would say I'd be banished to hell. I believe that hell is here on earth and it is what you make of it now or in the next life.

It is human to make mistakes, I have done things to be ashamed of but they do not control me anymore. The steps cleanse you and take you out of that darkness.

An open mind is what I pray for.

I pray that I lay aside everything I think I know about this disease, about the meetings, about myself, about other people and about God. For an open mind and a new experience with all these things.

I pray for that because it is my closed mindedness, my previous beliefs, my parents' conditioning that are going to hinder me from blossoming, growing and changing. You can't change your behaviours if you don't change your mind.

Those static firm beliefs aren't going to help me change anything or they would have already.

If you have an open mind, anything is possible!

That's what I've seen and experienced anyway.

I see people and they are so absolutely broken. They sit for a year and they won't do the steps. It's really sad. They look grey, miserable and depressing to talk to.

If you say to them, "Hey! There's a way out of all your problems. All you need to do is the twelve steps and believe in a Higher Power!" They look at you as if you've told them to jump off a cliff. And I get that. That was me. My head was strong on that one.

Because, excuse the crude saying, shit is warm and you don't know how to be any other way. You don't have the power and cannot even fathom being any other way. You don't want to be happy flappy 'seemingly controlled or brain washed' but that has what has made me freer than anything and now years on I do not need the meetings as much as in the beginning, they give you a bridge to normal living again.

It's a difficult one as you can't just 'give it to somebody', they need to be willing.

The rehab made us go to a meeting for homeless people. I think it was meant to scare us but for me it did the opposite, it alienated me. Making me feel inferior compared to the level they had gone!

These brave, lovely people were homeless, had been crack & heroin addicts for years, lost everything, nearly died. I found it very much like 'Well, I'm not as bad as that guy. I haven't lost everything, I'm not out on the street, I haven't got a needle in my arm. I can't be an addict. I must be fine.'

It was the perfect excuse for me. It made me want to do more drugs and get to an even worse state. That's how my addict mind works.

I found home in the meetings when I returned to France and met people my own age who'd done similar things in their life.

It didn't mean I wanted to do recovery. I had to become much more desperate before I came to that awakening.

9. Lizbeth's breakdown

So Meath was back in the rehab safe! Nearer me, that felt better... but did it?

I had to let go of worrying about everything, leave everything to the experts. I could do no more.

I would pace around the house, walk the dogs and feel empty, muddled, making excuses to a few friends not to go out with them.

Thinking, wondering, wandering, in my own world of despair.

I found myself crying and crying. Shutting the front door, locking it and having a slight feeling of some safety.

I'd put on the television but not listen to the words.

Watching familiar faces, faces of actors from my youth. Westerns were my favourites.

My brother and I were brought up on a farm north of Dublin, playing outside, cowboys and Indians and we always loved Westerns. I seemed to need old memories and home comfort.

I was so frightened inside.

I withdrew to my depths of the unexplained, the despairing questions which couldn't be answered.

How had our life come to this? Had it crept up quietly or suddenly? It was there and just didn't go away.

When had it all started?

It was so long since Meath and I had had relaxed happy times.

I blamed myself. Why couldn't I make her better? Why couldn't I help?

I thought I had been a good parent, friend, so why couldn't I do more now? My thoughts went from self-criticism to endless self-blame.

I would get up in the morning, walk the dogs, rush home, lock the doors quickly after myself, and pretend I was alright. I had always been a strong person and could tackle most people and problems. I would be the one helping friends, solving problems.

I didn't dare ring a good pal I had back home in Ireland. I felt ashamed. I believed maybe it was my fault. How does one start to explain and start the conversation that my daughter is in a rehab! And then continue to explain something I didn't know what I was talking about. The confusion. I felt like I needed someone, but who? My immediate family had left this world.

I couldn't see the mess I was in myself.

I existed from one day to the next in a sort of daze, feeling safe behind my bolted doors. Staring out the window, often with pouring silent tears.

My little four pawed friends nearby. I needed them, their friendly faces always loyal, looking at me helplessly.

I found I couldn't read anything. I had no ability to absorb any understanding. I couldn't get passed the first few words of any book or magazine. My concentration to understand the words was useless, everything seemed pointless. Everything else outside my world seemed trivial. My brain was blocked as if in permanent numbness.

I cried and cried, unable to leave home for long, feeling frightened, unable of holding a conversation.

So I sat in my blur, tears streaming down my face.

I made excuses to the few friends I had in France whom I normally saw and had a small social life with occasionally. I'd say I was out with the other friends, or invent silly stories not to see anyone.

I did try once to see some friends for dinner. I drove myself as I didn't want to drink because I became upset quickly. I thought I could enjoy the evening and forget for a bit. Half way through the meal, I became very choked up, and couldn't speak, or explain myself and had to leave quickly. One friend was very cross with me and sent me a rude email saying how dare I just walk out. I sent apologies but couldn't explain my inner turmoil or the situation.

I thought, never again. I wasn't ready, I just couldn't keep a conversation going without my worries intruding. Trite everyday talk seemed so superfluous compared with what was going on in my life. I must have panicked, so I fled.

I spent my time crying, hating myself, hating this situation, hating the world.

I had lost all my confidence. If anyone spoke to me in a shop I couldn't answer them. One day, after a shop assistant asked a simple question, I had to run home without my groceries, slam and lock the door. Relief, locked in, some safety. I felt constantly exhausted. No groceries, but I didn't care.

I told myself I was fine, Meath was being taken care of, I could garden, walk the dogs and that was plenty in my life, nature and my little pals.

What had I done wrong, or right, or what hadn't I done?

I had given a home, schooling, food, support, love. Had I been too indulgent? Can you be too loving and caring? Too much of a friend? Perhaps that was it.

I should have just not bothered so much and just let her get on with life.

Where had twenty odd years gone? How could I not have prevented this? Why me? Why us? Why anyone? I tormented myself.

When we'd had a difficult time in the past, I would suggest to Meath, 'Let's go away for a day or two'. Now it was she who said 'It's time to face this'. Every time we go away the problem is still there when we come back home.

When would our life change? I poured a drink, lit a cigarette and hid at home in tears. Nothing helped.

I felt weak, vulnerable, utterly and despairingly exhausted.

I was in a constant state of shock, standing alone in the world in solitary inexplicable numbness.

I meandered around in solitary absentmindedness for weeks until our Sunday afternoons would arrive.

After no contact all week, I'd be nervous, desperate to hug her. Wishing for the impossible magic wand to take this nightmare away.

It was peaceful, surreal, it just didn't seem like I was visiting my daughter in a drug rehabilitation clinic.

Meath puffed away and would talk about her week. She wanted to leave, complained about most of the procedure but seemed to be in a sort of acceptance at the same time. She was in her own world of learning, her programme of treatment. Her world of trouble.

I felt removed and felt her distance, maybe it was a sort of self-protection.

I left. Empty, alone, needing to bolt home and get behind that locked door.

Our weeks blurred like this for a month.

One Sunday we were let out for a walk and cup of tea. We chatted about nothing, empty things. I loved going to see her but felt totally left out of her life, I understood nothing.

As much as I wished to be with Meath I couldn't help that feeling of running home to safety.

This was my life of emptiness.

On one of my visits Meath suddenly said, "Ma you need help."

I let the idea sit in my brain. 'I' needed help! Where from?

Meath continued, "I know of someone in the next town and apparently he is a counsellor and does hypnosis treatment."

I could see Meath was becoming more positive in herself.

I was still in my muddy hell.

"Why, have you been talking about me?"

"Yes," she replied. "At some point they like to involve the whole family."

Later she rang me at home with a phone number of this counsellor. Meath was allowed her mobile for an hour each evening now.

I called and went for my first appointment.

Nervously I arrived and we had a chat regarding myself and Meath's addiction, what little I knew. I related many of the traumas of the last few years. For me, he said, he could help with meditative hypnosis and in a few weeks, I could bring my daughter in for hypnosis treatment. Professing he could cure her without the rehab programme.

I listened, it all sounded amazing. I, of course, had tears pouring down my face, like a steady flow. This was the first time I had spoken the truth about my despairing years and felt he might understand.

I told him about our difficult years, Meath's crazy years, with the result of becoming a drug addict. These words, 'drug addict', sort of stuck in my throat and still do. I poured out my loneliness since losing my parents and then in this last year, my brother, and how I felt so alone.

We went into a quiet room and I listened to meditation music of deep relaxation. The peace helped. When I left his room his parting words were, "When you stop the tears, you should go on a singles cruise."

Was he completely mad, I thought. As if having a man in my life with my troubles would help. I could hardly go to a shop, let alone go cruising with happy chatty people. At least not now.

The second therapist I was recommended was a slick forceful American lady, who wanted me to fill in endless forms about all my family members, all our medical history, asking the most probing questions and wanting to put me on an expensive course of appointments. She told me to go on her website, sign up and pay up. I found her knowledgeable but too stern and abrasive for my delicate condition. I felt my troubled mind was like a specimen to her, and I didn't feel comfortable with her regimented specific route of action. In fact, I found it very scary.

One day I was talking to Meath about this 'help' I needed, by this time we were allowed regular evening chats. She was sounding stronger and more informed by the week.

Suddenly she said, "You know the lady here called Neelam, who you first spoke to to get me into this place, is a therapist."

No, I wasn't aware of this. I was quite glad they, at the rehab, hadn't actually pushed me into this information right away. Refreshingly non-money-orientated.

I tentatively rang her and her wonderful calm voice said of course she would see me and asked whether I would write down all the traumas I'd had in my life to give her and we made an appointment.

A trauma list. I wasn't really sure what a trauma was, so she told me: death, divorce, moving house, severe illnesses, bumps to the head, prison, loss. I wrote them out and filled in her form. It was quite a long list, which I hated doing as I am a private person and like to forget troubles in life and keep moving onwards. The odd thing was I'd always thought I'd had a pretty wonderful life, keeping positive with thoughts of how lucky I was. Neelam said if I hadn't had this optimism, I probably would have topped myself by now, with all my traumas!

I seemed to be oblivious to the fact she said I was in the middle of a breakdown.

Breakdown, I thought, was for wimps. Apparently, I wasn't giving this breakdown the respect it needed.

Surely not a strong person like me? But right now, I was falling the hardest.

We would talk me with my sobs relating my last few years of loss, divorce, addiction, Meath and my life for the last several years. (I yearned to stop crying and be stronger.)

Neelam went slowly. I knew, at last, I was with the right person. We talked like good friends. I soon began to trust her completely. The costs were fair, she didn't push for lots of appointments and was always on the end of the phone should I need.

She explained that my traumas had built up until my body and mind finally now needed care, rest, time to understand and repair. That my mind and body had had enough stress and tension.

She ended our last few minutes asking what I was doing for me this evening, tomorrow or at the weekend. For me? I silently shouted in my head. I'm fine, just please help me understand Meath's problem and what's going on. Help Meath in here then all will be ok*ay*.

She wanted me to care for me, eat good food, rest, sleep, only see or talk to trusted old friends. If I only felt like staying in and watching television, then only do that. "Nurture yourself," she'd say. "You're in a breakdown, you are overwhelmed."

Yes, I was overwhelmed. It seemed to perfectly describe my mind.

I learnt one day at a time - if I felt fragile, don't push myself, rest, rest, rest.

I'd found a trusted friend in her, a good person who taught me so much.

First about how to strengthen myself, then about Meath's addiction.

I had to face the learning, the understanding of us both, for us both.

I thought I could learn it quickly and then get on with our lives.

No, this was not possible. It had to become part of our life.

I withdrew further from friends, acquaintances.

If a friend had told me I would one day end up in therapy I definitely wouldn't have believed them. I am, or was, the most grounded level-headed strong person.

The first therapy appointment was not as I imagined one would be. Neelam met me as I walked up the garden to the rehab house. I instinctively looked out for Meath. Nowhere in sight. I missed her very much.

We made a cup of tea in the office and walked around to a side room where we sat and just started chatting. No couch or stern faces, just a kind face in a small friendly room.

I said I'd really like to understand as much as possible about addiction and what was going on with us both.

I can't remember in which order... but she started... Explaining that…

I was the enabler.

Dear God, what a name. It sounded like another wrong, another bloody label, another self-punishment which I took on board in my fragile brain. Something else to blame on myself.

So yes, then I could see I had been enabling my daughter to carry on with her addiction by providing a home, paying her debts, and fundamentally not chucking her out of the house.

I should have cast her out and shut the front door.

Really! Can anyone? "Yes," said Neelam. She had had to do this to her child. Eventually.

Then Meath's rock bottom demise would probably have come sooner if I'd had the balls to shut the door on my child. And 'I' had helped Meath NOT get to rock bottom sooner.

Paying, caring, loving, wishing, hoping.

I couldn't have shut her out of our home, close my purse, my door, my life, my mind, my mother's heart.

I inwardly defended myself but the reality was there for me to see now.

"This ain't no phase any longer, it's gone on too long!"

Now here we were.

Both in treatment!

Neelam said Meath should be paying for this treatment herself! I was surprised.

I told her she had some money which her grandparents had left her. So I arranged to use this. I felt terrible. I had already paid the first month but it was Meath's learning to help her understand the value of money. It seemed severe but I trusted this place by now, they were helping us both. She would then have more respect, value and get more out of the rehab learning. Part of the growing up process.

Neelam told me how when Meath arrived that her addiction age was only about fourteen or fifteen years old, she was actually twenty-five. Already in one month she had grown in two to three years of knowledge and awareness, without drugs and their teaching.

When Meath left after three months she had 'grown' by six aware years of maturity. The fast track of learning in the right rehab.

Now I was beginning to understand why my bright intelligent daughter couldn't seem to progress in life. Forever seeming like the wild child.

Addiction 'gets in the way' of thinking normally, learning, keeping a job.

Always the obsessive mind taking over their thoughts and actions. She would start a project off very well, 'great promise' would be on the school report – 'has great potential'. But slowly the reports were less enthusiastic.

Sometimes it was hard to hold a conversation with Meath. I could see her mind was elsewhere.

Neelam explained that when Meath started to get clean, the most important thing was to just stay clean for one day at a time, one hour, one minute. Just for today, "I will try to live through this minute, this hour..." It was too overwhelming to think of being clean any more than that.

The addict's obsessive mind can make even the smallest task excruciating when they are not using for the first few months. They live in a mental battle with themselves so it can be a slow process to get well and living having to only think about staying clean for today makes it much easier on the mind. .

We can't plan tomorrow. We need patience.

I wasn't to expect a lot from her too soon and I must learn how to deal with me.

So just for this minute, my today, I will adjust and have patience that she is on the right path and proceeds as slowly as is needed. I found it difficult.

I learned how difficult it must have been for Meath to study at school, to look after herself or concentrate on anything for too long. Her mind was far too busy fighting with the voices of addiction. At school she could have been seen as time wasting, an underachiever, or… the other way I believe it goes – overachieving until burnt out. Addicted to work. Never good enough. Unhappy with low self-worth... The obsessive racing mind can dismiss their chance of growing up, achieving, being responsible or stunt them from enjoying life by thinking only of work, body image, money etc. If left unnoticed, untreated it turns to anger, drink, drugs, eating disorders, obsessions, irritability, dissatisfaction, low concentration.

Now Meath would learn at the start to do a good deed and learn to care for herself – to do two things she didn't really want to do –keep her voice low, try and be tidy, clean, polite and not be critical. She had a lot of 'work' to do, Neelam said.

Just for today, she will start and grow...

I couldn't take in all of Neelam's advice and information – it was drip fed over many sessions.

What I couldn't compute in my exhausted mind is why addicts are supposed to be and are, such intelligent bright people. If so, why can't they stop after one or two glasses of wine. Why the whole bottle? Why the stronger or stronger drug, until floored?

Their mind is blocked in this regard.

In an addict's mind, they can't stop thinking about that drink or drug, morning, noon and night. Magnify this 1,000 times in a day. How do you suppose you can get anything done? Some voice gnawing away in your head. You can't concentrate, can't think... Poor me, pour me a drink, pour me another and another, give me the bottle... Stop the voices... the worry, the anxiety. Like a moth to a flame.

It's understandable, isn't it? A chink of dawning in my brain.

Neelam advised to not be so hard on myself, that I am human, I'm allowed to cry. I'm allowed to feel upset and I can take my time to repair. It was understandable that I was in this breakdown. I can allow myself all the time I need. At last, some kind understanding.

I remember asking a few really stupid questions at the beginning of some sessions, like...

Meath would never be able to drink again! "What, not even one glass?" but I thought, *she is a drug addict, not an alcoholic?*

"The addiction of one rapidly leads to the other," was the reply, and then she'd be back on drugs.

"Not even one glass of champagne when she gets married or has her first baby?" I asked.

"No," was her strong answer.

Why had I asked such an ignorant question? Why on earth did it seem important to clink glasses to celebrate a marriage or birth or at a meal. All I should have been thinking of was Meath was alive and we could clink glasses with water. Didn't sound the same mentally.

Now we do, happily.

It's a conditioning of the mind of years of doing the same thing, for generations even and I've learned I can have fun and a very happy time without the accustomed glass of alcohol. I can clink glasses and say cheers to Meath with a smile of gratitude, with a glass of water.

I was advised it doesn't matter whether it takes one day or years to become stronger again. That everyone who suffers loss, traumas, addiction, their healing, understanding and rewiring are different.

This gave me permission to stop beating myself up wondering why I couldn't pick myself up more quickly. So I relaxed into these enlightening words and felt better. I can take my time, no one is judging me or expecting anything from me.

I'd understand this addiction better through time, especially as I become stronger.

Day by day, this seemed acceptable, bearable, do-able.

So I learnt I could only 'change me'.

All the motherly advice and cajoling in the world with Meath would never have got me anywhere with her addiction.

I had to learn to change me. Only me.

You can't change anyone else.

Oh yes, we think we might be able to nag, persuade, bully, bribe, charm, ask 'please do it, for me, at least'! We think we are trying to 'help' them but unless a person wants to change they just won't or can't.

We are only responsible for ourselves.

I learnt addiction is a disease... Yes, a dis-ease, out of ease with your mind. Out of ease with yourself, uneasy inside.

I thought of 'disease' as a frightening word, linked to cancer, leukaemia, AIDS, maladies which are 'seen' as an illness. Physical visible illness. Helped, hopefully, with cures, medicines, hospitals and doctors.

You can't see addiction in most people.

Plus, in general people think it's the person, the addict's fault.

10. Meath. Active addiction

Living with the active disease of addiction, when your tolerance to your substance builds so strong that the drug/alcohol effect no longer works and you can no longer numb yourself (AKA the drugs don't work anymore), is the scariest, most torturous feeling... That there's not enough, you can't get enough to satisfy, so you substitute with other drugs and alcohol to numb the insatiable craving, the allergy for more but all you want is your drug of choice, or your drug of no choice. Your number 1 lover over ANY other.

Craving it with every cell in your body, the beast needs to be fed, we are taken over and nothing can shut up the voices for MORE... Like the need for air that we breathe. Like a fish out of water, ripping your heart out of your chest as it breaks and you are so aware of your hopelessness and the terror and realisation of the monster that you are and what you need slaps you in the face with utter powerlessness and complete obsession and despair.

There is no answer, just more. More, more!

You know you need to stop for a while to build your tolerance back but you can't stop, so you keep using but to no effect until you want to kill yourself. Drinking bottles of cough syrup out of the cupboard and searching old clothes pockets... Crumbs on the carpet... That was me.

The world becomes grey and unrecognisable. Nothing else matters. You are a shell of a being, completely dead of spirit, without soul, without joy. Not even the sunshine can warm you. The world is sour, bitter and against you. You vs the world, with your only saviour being a drug that is killing you. Robbing you of life, love, any goodness. You are alone, just like it wants- your addict. You know what it's doing but the superhuman strength is unconquerable. The disease of addiction is stronger than man. It takes no prisoners, waits for no one, hides in the shadows to break you, tear your family apart, lie, cheat, steal. Keep you there on the floor where you belong with the dirt, while it feeds from you and your soul like the Grim Reaper.

When you are in this state you are not in denial. You are in complete delusion.

Because the disease centres in the mind, it tricks you and lies to you, so you can no longer trust your own thoughts. The addict's brain is not well, not sane. Polluted. And the addict, although aware there is a problem, cannot connect with the truth and facts of the matter enough to be able to stop.

There are some that can stop for a while but right there I am talking about fierce addiction when you are in it and there is no way out.

On paper, the drug I was addicted to isn't physically addictive like heroin or cocaine but if you are that way disposed, damaged in the way that you cannot live life without some kind of buffer, some way to numb, take the edge off, it is just as mentally addictive as crack cocaine.

No common acknowledgement of the disease conversation.

Meath: "You can see why people don't buy into the disease of alcoholism."

Lizbeth: "Because it's such hard work to stay on the straight and narrow?"

Meath: "Because if the 'addict person' is not what the other understands as visibly ill (as is with a disease like cancer or AIDS, when physically you can see the person in front of you is ill).

The mad thing is the addict alcoholic does look ill but people don't view it as that. They see drinking as a choice, (as it is for them, per say) they believe he's doing that to himself. It's a bit like allergies – people who don't have them just don't understand."

Lizbeth: "Plus, others think, *If he's got any brains then why hasn't he got the intelligence to stop himself*?"

Meath: "Yes, it's like blaming the cancer patient for eating bad food, smoking, drinking to excess but people just don't see it like that."

Lizbeth: "They don't associate a bad diet or too much drinking with an illness, as when we're young we think we'll live forever, drink smoke and be merry. You don't think of your lungs, heart or what poison you're throwing inside for your body to cope with."

Meath: "They just don't see drinking as an illness, because I guess there's proof… in cancer or whatever, there it is proof, the doctor shows you test results...

But if an alcoholic or addict goes to most doctors with drinking there's no X-ray or test. They may say, 'Oh well, you've got depression or this and this is happening in your life, which is making you drink.' You lost your job, your husband beat you, your wife left you and gives you an excuse like you were abused, that's all the reasons why you drink, that's why and when you are better you will be okay. A bit of therapy, some pills etc."

Lizbeth: "It's the excuse you give yourself to drink or take drugs."

Meath: "The doctor should know to ask, does your mind do this, does your body need this after a few drinks?

Well, then they could diagnose the disease of addiction and recommend recovery or tell them what to look out for as traits.

So many people say only an alcoholic can say if he is an alcoholic but I personally think if somebody's brains are so addled with alcoholism, they can't actually put up their hand and say 'Yes, I am' because they have an obsessive mind which is full of denial which is the only way they can carry on. So the person who's in complete delusion and denial cannot then say, 'Yes, it's me I'm an alcoholic.' They're never going to say that they're in denial! The whole disease is telling them they need to drink to survive.

Someone else has to do that. If people like doctors and nurses were armed with the truth about this it would be so helpful.

But we're very young in the world. It's only been since 1930`s when the big book was written and then, there were only a handful of people in America who knew anything about it. We're still very young in our knowledge."

Lizbeth: "And it's not accepted as a medical disease."

Meath: "It is some places but yes not others."

Lizbeth: "There's no financial help for anybody."

Meath: "I've been to see so many doctors, so many people, because at the end of the day, the addict/alcoholic will ALWAYS try to seek out anything but having to stop taking alcohol or drugs.

I'd say I'd like to take something for depression, I'd like to take pills, I'd like to see a therapist and I'd prefer to take anything but stop taking a drink or drug.

Most doctors I've seen say it's circumstances, you'll grow out of it, it's a phase. And I'm sure that is the case with people who have a bad experience and go a little overboard but you need to know the full truth and story. Get to the bottom of what makes you tick."

Lizbeth: "Just as I thought when you were a teenager."

Meath: "The doctor or therapist could say you just need to get into a good relationship or get a good job, things like that, and it will be okay. You get all your ducks in a row and you'll be fine. Well, all my ducks were in a row and I was never fine."

Silence.

11. More therapy for Lizbeth

I arrived one afternoon to see Neelam, feeling a little freer in my mind. I seemed to be offloading and it was obviously working, as some positivity was returning in my mind.

Talking was helping, a rarity for me.

We chatted for a while then she suddenly gave me the news that Meath had a boyfriend.

I was very surprised.

Oh no, no.

Turmoil of words whirled round my head. Why on earth did she need a boyfriend now. Couldn't she, for once in her life, concentrate and just get on with learning what she needed for now? The distraction of a boyfriend irritated me. I couldn't see how this would help, only hinder her progress.

Neelam went on to say he's been clean for three years. Clean! He's also an addict. Drug addict daughter, addict boyfriend, where were all these addicts coming from and how did she meet him!

"Where did she meet him?" I blurted out.

"At the meetings in the last few weeks."

Oh, the horror of it all, I thought. More problems.

More mental exhaustion overwhelmed me.

I knew what Meath was like with boyfriends. She would be totally immersed and sometimes obsessed in a relationship.

Oh, the confusion of an affair.

Neelam reassured me that she could benefit from his experience, with his knowledge and support.

I wouldn't realise for a long while that his input to her learning would be such a great help.

I accepted this bit of news, negativity washing over me.

Neelam stressed the importance of looking after me. Which I forget over and over again.

She tried to explain that the 'clan' (a nickname I used as I couldn't get myself to say addicts) learned to cope, learned from their support group, learned from their sponsors and sponsees, their new friends and meetings.

Then the family member of the addict, or boyfriend/girlfriend, gets left behind in a heap of exhaustion and confusion. Perhaps having lost all your friends, lost the energy to get going in life again. Lost the will or enthusiasm to do anything.

You are physically and mentally wrung out.

I now started to understand why she said at the end of each session *and what are you doing for you this tonight? Cook a favourite meal, ring a good friend. Watch your favourite film. Do something you enjoy. Nurture 'you'.*

I understand now that when your loved one progresses and gets stronger to fight this addiction, they are moving on with their group, getting better.

You are left behind, and it's a lonely place to be left in.

You have given all your energy, love, reserves and emotions into trying to look after the 'troubled' member in your family. They progress, but there is suddenly nothing left for you.

All these years I'd forgotten myself quite a lot.

At least that happened to me.

I was certainly shattered. Restarting some sort of social or working life seemed impossible, unimportant and daunting. Everything seemed impossibly difficult.

I had learnt to deflect the usual normal questions about Meath from friends, family and just say she was fine. You could look at her pretty face, looking normal, carry on a great conversation but what goes on behind the facade, inside, was unexplainable.

Yes, I avoided questions, avoided meeting anyone.

53

If you don't learn to care for you, you won't get stronger, you will be left behind, and it's a solitary place to be left in, at least for too long.

It's taken me six years to really feel confident again. Talk to others, walk tall into a room, not cry from the memories of despair. To look someone in the eye and carry on a conversation.

Not to feel so bloody fragile.

I've become a calmer person, a much more understanding person of my pain and others' pain. This book is about us giving back our experience, our knowledge. If anyone reading this relates to our words, sees similarities and can believe in the hope, that there is hope and there could be help and a better life with an addict in your life, then writing this has been worthwhile.

My life has changed so very much, the importance of things has changed, my value of material things. Small talk with friends has become trivial. I seem to appreciate more meaningful pursuits and values.

Meetings for Meath, I learned, for her became very important, where they met like-problemed people, where they shared their desperate stories, where they related and supported each other in total privacy.

Meath made friends there, not just her boyfriend. Other girls with similar addictions. I learnt they helped one another with everyday things, moving homes, trying to find work, difficulty with a car that wouldn't start. There would be a clan member who would help another. A great support for one another.

I learnt it was an achievement to go to these meetings at first and that Meath would resist sometimes until it became almost part of her life. Certainly, if she appeared angry and quarrelsome during the week, after a meeting she would be calmer and have less inner stress. She started to find it easier making friends, contacts, learning, growing.

While me... day by day – actually, it was year by year – I was taking a long time to be able to go out and face the world and suddenly I saw my empty calendar and the empty life of despair I'd been in. The huge plus was we were both getting better slowly.

Meath was now on the way and surely, I could follow.

It's too difficult to explain over a cup of tea with a friend or family member what's been going on. You could talk yourself into knots defending your addict's condition and illness.

I tried one day with a close friend but she just kept asking more questions, all the time the non-belief in her voice. That an intelligent girl could not just stop.

All my answers just went straight over her head. I shut up. What was the point? I could feel instinctively her thoughts were that I'd spoilt her!

I fumed inside, at my own inadequacy of my not being able to explain correctly, or her obstinacy at not understanding. I had to stop my inner defensive thoughts.

After all, it had taken me many appointments with Neelam, months of learning, years of acceptance and listening to believe this is a disease.

But most importantly...

IT IS NOT THEIR FAULT.

This knowledge helped me hugely.

No control over an unseen enemy.

Over the years I'd made taped feelings and thoughts of my experiences. These have helped put together several pages in this book.

I was shocked at my voice. It was so slow, so traumatised. I heard a lot of pain and exhaustion in it. I obviously was a victim at that time. Not just Meath as the 'ill' one, I had become mentally and physically 'ill'.

I am no longer a victim.

I think I'd always thought addicts were people who had no hope, no money, no home, no will to live, no ambition. Just didn't care for anything. And no one to care and love them.

Maybe come from an abusive family, were very poor and were in so much despair they turned to drugs or alcohol.

Meath had had love, family, a home and care. Addiction is indiscriminate in who it chooses and can maybe even be passed down from family members. There seems to be no medical proof of this but an addiction tendency can show up from one member in a family to another and not necessarily be the same addiction. A parent may be an alcoholic and their child could have an eating disorder or have obsessive cleaning disorder, or obsessive gambling.

Meath, in this rehab, would learn from watching others in front of her, how they behaved, talked and listen to their horror stories, hear their anger and fears.

Find similarity of experiences not differences. Learn by example.

Choose for herself, realise maybe she was an addict and what to do about it, for herself.

When the time came for Meath to leave, Neelam suggested she go to America, to a clinic where they pioneered this recovery procedure and where they were having amazing success.

Meath dug her heels in, she wanted to be here, at home, near her boyfriend, and insisted she could learn all the rest from going to meetings.

I was nervous but gave in. My instincts wanted her near anyway. Good sense told me she would be better and quicker recovery in the US. We would see.

Time shows, time cures, time helps.

One chat session, Neelam gave me a book about having the courage to change... myself.

More to do, more of me.

I left that session feeling flat. It seemed like another mountain to climb.

However...

There were 365 pages with a wonderful reading on each page for your day. I would let the book fall at whichever page it wanted and read slowly. I'd have to read it several times to absorb it.

These words showed a bit of light and I started reading a page now and then each morning.

Give me patience, this was no fast track.

12. Lizbeth chats with Neelam

I was learning from Neelam that addiction could be hereditary. She asked me if there were any family I remembered or knew of who were alcoholics or drug addicts or had any other obsessive behaviours.

I recalled a distant cousin my mother had told me about, who was an alcoholic and had died with holes in her jumpers and empty gin bottles in her dustbins.

On one of my regular visits with Neelam, she said that their rehab was having a family weekend. She would very much like me to attend.

The weekend would be for any family member of an addict, or a girlfriend/boyfriend could join in the whole weekend in which there would meeting sessions – sometimes just us and other times when we'd all be together in a general meeting of addicts, the present inmates, therapists and us.

It sounded like the worst nightmare of all her ideas. She said it was beneficial to all and we'd learn a lot.

There were several things we had to prepare.

We, on both sides, had to write down our personal complaints, accusations, affirmations of how we wanted to live our lives in the future, which we would speak directly aloud to our addict loved one.

We would say exactly how we felt and what we wanted to change in our lives.

We, the family, would be asked to sign a form saying we wouldn't take any drugs or alcohol for the lead up to the week and for the weekend.

I was frightened and horrified. The only glimmer of silver lining I could see was the fact my ex couldn't join us that weekend. He would go another time. I doubted that.

I now knew Meath wasn't to blame and had learnt quite a lot, so why did we have to go through this scene, this big vision of upset emotions and accusations?

I felt horrorstruck and sick with apprehension.

Would this demand of me never end?

I would be there on my own with the other families. It was to last three days, from about 10.00 a.m. until 5.00 p.m.

I chose to blank it out and just go at the appointed hour. I felt very fragile.

I organized myself to walk my dogs early. Tried to mentally prepare.

It felt like a never-ending horror epic.

13. Lizbeth. Family weekend... some weekend

I was distraught before I left home, for days leading up to it.

I wasn't confident of my emotions, or how I would react.

I felt Meath and I were already doing enough, it was hard work and stressful, for me anyway and now more.

Always more.

I don't think Neelam really understood what an ordeal this would be for me.

With a huge apprehensive feeling of dread and nervousness, I parked the car and slowly made myself walk up the driveway. My feet were like concrete but I plodded on resolutely. I had parked on the road outside, ready for escape.

I was shown into a room with the other family members of the other inmates in the clinic.

Inmates seemed gentler than addicts. I hated that word. Such a harsh label.

We were in one room and in the connecting room I could hear Meath and her 'friends' chatting. Giving an air of a surreal congenial coffee morning.

I felt apart and saw Meath was in her own separateness from me, with her comrades in understanding. Dealing with this day in their way.

I felt alone. Lost. Way out of my depth. I wanted to run back to the car and flee.

My feet were heavy but kept me there like a dutiful parent. I nodded and tried to acknowledge the others, but not with a smile. I couldn't trust myself to speak.

The meeting started and we all sat down in a circle, them and us.

There were times when Meath and the others went out, times when we had lectures on the different phases of addiction and recovery, helping us to try and understand. They showed us a sort of a downward graph of using drugs/alcohol, broken in deep addiction, levelling off and then the hopeful upward line of expected learning to recovery.

Once, there was the accusation moment, a very upsetting time, when Meath and I sat in chairs opposite each other, quite closely, with everyone around us watching, listening.

We 'told' the other what we didn't like about our life with each other and the present situation, how each of us wanted the future to be.

I remembered I said I could no longer have Meath in my home if she took drugs again, how she must look after herself, her room, her clothes, her life.

I stuttered this, not really feeling I meant it. I did, but I just wanted this all to go away and have a happy life. Neelam told me I had to be strong and say these things or we wouldn't progress.

Meath wouldn't get to long-term recovery if I was weak.

Meath told me I wasn't to keep ringing her, I had no right to move her possessions from Dublin back here to France, I had to stop worrying or she would move out, not to tell her what to do with her life. She said if I told her what to do she just wanted to do the opposite, I was to trust her.

I was shocked, I defended my actions in my mind. I was a caring, loving mother.

I felt sick to the pit of my stomach.

I found it hard to believe what I said I might have to put into reality.

This self-belief that 'I' could have helped my daughter to get better, was I suppose my delusion, I had to become tougher, stronger.

We were to become less co-dependent.

I didn't understand this meaning ago when Neelam had first used this word ages ago.

It meant I couldn't be happy unless Meath was happy.

I had to stop with the meals, roof over her head, loving help. I needed to be stronger, needed to be less motherly and loving, more like a school mistress or distant aunt, which for me conjured up a vision of not being me.

I had to change.

Neelam blatantly said if I didn't change and Meath continued and possibly relapsed in the future, she could kill herself. Addiction would kill her.

This sank into my depths of my fearful heart. I sat in a feeling of shock as I absorbed this.

I had to change. I would. My resolve was strong. I would change and do whatever I had to.

The fact I could lose her was a reality shock.

I had to be strong for us both.

Allow her to grow in her recovery. Not sit worrying. I must get over this breakdown, and get strong.

More, more, more, from me. Drained. Overwhelmed. Utterly exhausted.

But I would do it. I would. This was our survival.

During these accusations to each other, the others families, rehab therapists and other addicts listened to us, baring our lives in the open.

Then we listened to them in turn say their family's piece.

I was so exhausted from that and found it so intrusive, into the privacy of someone else's life's difficulties, I hardly listened.

I sat but couldn't hear the details, as if in my brain it was impolite to hear them and really these were secrets between them.

I was good at blocking what I didn't want to hear or couldn't cope with.

Is this the American way, one reads about? I never thought I'd be in the middle of a situation like this.

I'd been brought up in quite harmonious family life. The old-fashioned way, putting up, getting on.

I would realise, to talk was a good way to move forward, get results. Liberating and cleansing your mind of round and round thoughts and worries.

We had to draw pictures of how we viewed our home life now and a picture of how we would like it to be.

I drew a house with black clouds over it, rain and darkness inside, all doors and windows shut. Signifying the past.

The other house, our hope, with sunshine and the windows and doors open, with light and colour inside. The future.

Then we had to draw pictures of how we saw each other together in our life.

Meath drew two columns: us, standing strong together but independently strong, with smaller columns, our dogs by our side, in bright colours.

Which is where we are now. Nine years later... independent, together, apart, respectful of each other's life and space. Getting on with our own independent lives, lovingly and with a deep understanding and respect.

We can laugh again, we are friends. Happy.

There was a moment when I suffered terrible stomach pains. The lecturing therapist had taken my mind back to my married life, when my husband had bullied and hit me.

My inner pain, my inner shame and my humiliation was buried deep down inside.

When the recollection moved up to the surface, even a tiny bit of memory, the physical pain was immense. I had to leave the group and hide in a corner of the room, doubled up in anguish. I was glad Meath and her group were in another room.

I cried and became angry, saying I didn't want to go back there and remember. I didn't want to remember these episodes in my life.

I was angry with them – the therapist. Why did he push me to go back to my dark inner pain? I was also glad he, my ex, wasn't here to see this.

But there were other families in this group who were mentally cleansing themselves in front of each other, and saying the barest most honest factual appraisals of each other, then apologies and hugs.

I managed the long weekend ordeal, thankful that every night I could go back to my sanctuary, walk the dogs and the peace of my locked doors, wishing this weekend was over.

It did of course come to its last minute. I was physically and mentally shattered. I fled as soon as I could. I didn't see Neelam for a few weeks. I needed time to get over it all.

My ex for the family weekend.

About two months later my ex said he would come and stay and join the family clinic weekend.

I could hardly believe it. I never thought he would.

I wanted him to stay in a hotel nearby, as advised by Neelam, but he persuaded and nagged me into staying with me.

As I wanted to keep the peace, plus I also wanted him to come and learn as much as possible, I reluctantly agreed to him staying with me.

Could this be his enlightenment and his understanding? Maybe they would help him.

I was forever hopeful.

I felt I was moving forward, a bit stronger. I didn't want him to change his mind and not turn up. For all our sakes, I must get him here.

He signed the form not to take alcohol or anything during that week, but I didn't see him prepare any questions.

I drove him nervously every morning wondering how it would go.

Every evening I went to collect him. He would say, "They don't know what they're talking about. What a load of rubbish, waste of time and money."

He said Meath was fine, she was an intelligent girl, she should get out of that place and lead a normal life, and of course she could have a drink. She would know now not to do any more drugs. Drinking would be fine.

He just was not getting it.

Later, in a session with Neelam, she told me he was a completely deluded person. Deluded about himself and Meath's condition and most other things in life.

I told her that he took sleeping pills every night, and had a few glasses of wine most evenings during that family week. She was surprised.

He was above any requests he didn't want to do, a law unto himself. As always.

The morning he left for the airport, I had my speech prepared for him. I felt stronger.

I said he would no longer be welcome in my home. He wasn't ever to come back.

I'd arranged for him to be taken to the airport. I was not going to pander and be frightened of his ways anymore.

I was surprised at the strength in my words, but so sad, as he looked like the beaten child who didn't understand. He could sway from the angry bully, to this sad-eyed confused person. Which was how he'd kept me from walking out so many times.

The bullying during our marriage could carry on for weeks, until I could take no more. I would pack a bag, get to the door, then suddenly he would be kind, sorry, promising he would not shout, hit me or bully anymore.

For a week or so, it would be good. I would try extra hard, working to make our life as happy as possible. Then slowly or suddenly he would change. He'd have an angry moment driving home, blaming someone for driving badly, or have had an argument with someone in town. Somehow, he'd blame me, and I usually took it, trying to pacify him.

Some mornings I'd wake up to a happy man, others I'd wake up to anger and blame.

If things didn't go his way during the day, he would blow up, take a swing at me in the early days of marriage. Sometimes he would follow me as I ran upstairs to get away from him and he would corner me and kick me in the shins or hit my arms and back. All the while shouting it was all my fault with his angry red face close to mine. If I was pushed too far, I would shout back, defending myself, but I had to be pushed to my limit. I couldn't defend myself when he was really frightening. I was never sure whether to run or try to stand and argue back, whichever I chose seemed to be the wrong choice at that moment!

It either made him angrier or more violent.

Reasoning did not work, before, during or after an argument.

Sometimes it could take me days to pick myself up again, thinking this was the last straw, time to leave for good. He was clever, he seemed to know, would suddenly be nice, or smile or give me a hug and told me to cheer up, or turn the little lost boy look on. Which of course would melt my heart again and inside I promised myself I would try harder to make our marriage work.

If I ever tried to talk these times out with him, he would push the blame onto to me very quickly, walk away, or I'd see after about two minutes he couldn't concentrate on the conversation, ignore me and walk away.

I'd learnt after about ten years of marriage, if I needed to talk to him about anything serious, I needed to write a letter or note. This would give him time to reread and absorb slowly so hopefully not jump into his anger and not 'hear' me. He was unable to carry on a conversation, and if I couldn't get my point across right away, he would leave the room or snap.

I tried for many years to save our marriage, especially after Meath was born. I blamed myself and thought kindness, tolerance and love would win.

You see, I was in love with him, marriage and my home.

It was but an illusion.

When he was happy and in a good place, he was exciting company and a kind person inside… The person I'd fallen for.

The proverbial rapidly changeable Jekyll & Hyde.

I chose to always see the positive and good in people. I hoped and deeply believed I could make things better.

My family stopped visiting us and friends were either banned or wouldn't come by anymore. He would say they were boring and he didn't want to see anyone anyway.

I had slowly been losing my confidence. Sometimes I would ring a girlfriend and ask if I was really a bad person – that's how unsure of myself I became.

You see if you are hit, a lot or a little, you feel humiliated, to blame somehow. You do believe you are at fault and it's hard to explain to a friend as you believe they will think you drove him to lash out. Hard to win, so you put up and shut up.

I never knew when the last straw would arrive. I knew it would one day, sometimes I longed for it.

I also knew it would be very difficult for me to leave. I was brought up in a peaceful, loving family, I thought marriages were all the same and I could win over his anger.

I loved our home farm in mid-Ireland. I dreamt of bringing up Meath, surrounded with fields and animals, fresh air, family and love. It wasn't to be.

As Meath grew up, I saw she noticed the angry arguments. Once he got up from the kitchen table while I was washing up and hit me across the back of the head.

I reacted badly and shouted at him and quickly took the argument outside to protect Meath, but she had seen and heard.

That night when I tried to read her to sleep, I held her as she cried and I vowed to myself we had to go. I had a strong determined reason now. She was crying and didn't understand why. I needed to protect her.

My doctor said one of the worst things another person can do is to undermine their confidence. And my confidence was at rock bottom.

I had become brainwashed. He had been rude to so many of my friends, so we were leading a family solitary life.

I remember wishing to be the good wife and have a happy home. In the early days I would ask several of our friends for dinner, I would make everything, all homemade. I loved cooking. I'd plan and work for a week, and then I could see after about the main course he would look fidgety, looking out the window, turning up the music, then get up and tell everyone to f*** off.

I'd learn in my self-protection to block the scene out of my mind. The next day for him, it was as if nothing had happened.

There was no use talking about it – he'd just say he was bored or the friends were boring.

Needless to say, I 'lost' many friends. Later after we left, they came back into my life.

My mother said she wouldn't come over to the farm for meals any more or go out with him to a restaurant. She was a gentle soul and couldn't bear it if he was rude. He seemed happy to make a scene or be very rude, or ruin our meals with his complaining. I had constant indigestion.

At a restaurant, he couldn't seem to talk about anything with me for long. He'd look across the restaurant and if he saw someone smoking, he would glare at them all evening, or if someone was overweight or not attractive, he would then spend his time glaring at them, making loud comments, while I cringed and tried endlessly to find some topic to talk about to divert his attention. All pointless. My indigestion worsening. I must be a boring person to be with, I thought.

I steadily lost my confidence but believed I could make our marriage work. This was probably the stupid and silly reason I couldn't walk away earlier in the marriage – my stubbornness and insistence in the belief that I could resolve this difficulty.

You, the reader, are probably asking yourself why on earth I put up with this life for over twenty years. Well, I'm quite old-fashioned. I believed marriage was forever, a Catholic, my parents had had such a happy life and I ever hoped we could.

Then, a nun at the church I went to occasionally, said, "God didn't mean you to put up with this." I hadn't told her, but she'd seen my state when I'd go to church.

Also, my doctor said I could become seriously ill if I put up with this much longer.

So I had my 'permission'.

I was a fairly intelligent and capable woman – why did I need this confirmation and permission to leave? I seemed to need this reality from others to show me I couldn't repair it. I had to see the truth through others' opinions.

Then suddenly I realised he could never ever be happy inside himself. That was the key to his inner turmoil.

No matter what I did he was not happy. This I couldn't cure.

This was my last straw.

I planned our departure. It took me many months to pull it off as amicably as possible! Of course, this took me a while.

We, Meath and I and a few others, had started karate classes many months previously. I believed that my daughter should never be with a partner who would hit her and I wanted her to be able to protect herself, feel an inner strength. It was a great exercise and discipline. Somehow, it started to give me an inner confidence. As I managed to prove to myself one day, I had a breakthrough.

I was in our garden and asked if I could change some shrubs. He stormed over to me in his farm boots, red face, I knew that look. The usual angry words of, "F... off if you don't like it, this is 'my' home."

But instead of being frightened, and I don't know where the strength came from, I jumped out of the flower bed, fists clenched and yelled at him, "Don't you f****** dare ever hit me again." I was suddenly so furious at his injustice.

He stopped in his tracks, turned and walked away.

I was amazed. At his reaction and myself!

I ran to the garage and got on my bicycle and peddled down the drive and cycled away. I cycled for ages. I was shaking.

I couldn't believe myself. I smiled, felt elated. My confidence grew.

Then realisation, I'd left with nothing, (days before mobiles), no money.

Well, I had to go home. His home.

I peddled back into the farmyard, looking around. Scared of seeing him again. Could I stand up to him again?

I eventually saw him and he acted like it had never happened.

I had lived in a misty world of romantic hope. But no more.

I didn't know then my husband had an eating disorder, and controlled his obsessive mind with his temper. Yes, he was an addict as well, but obsessed about his weight and controlled himself with anger and delusion.

Enlightenment. I've just realised, as I write this story and think back, most of his temper and dissatisfaction seemed to be at mealtimes!

Now I've learnt, his mind constantly obsessing, not being able to hold a conversation for long with anyone. His low concentration levels, his obsessive mind troubles, eating disorders, anger issues, all left untreated would grow into an unhappy solitary life, while deluding himself he is perfect.

Time... I stopped giving excuses for him.

Time I woke up... my last straw had finally arrived, he would never be happy inside.

Time to leave 'his home', as he always called it, so Meath and I left.

As a few years passed by, Meath started her 'early teenage disruptions', I'll call them for now. She then went to Dublin to boarding school.

As there was nothing left for me in the country – no marriage, no close family, my nearest had departed this world. I decided to move to France. Start again! New horizons.

I had thought her difficult teenage years were because of our divorce.

How life can change almost without you realising.

It sort of evolved slowly and one day I awoke and we were in therapy, en France.

I had been living in my dream world.

Where had happiness and laughter gone?

14. Meath Family Therapy Weekend

I remember being told about the family therapy weekend. Instant fear came. I argued that I would only do it if they didn't invite my father. He would never understand I told them, it would be of no benefit other than to upset me. He wouldn't listen and he wouldn't hear anything. But they had never met my father and so they didn't understand.

They agreed he didn't have to come but little did I know they were just waiting for a later time to make me agree.

I was more excited to see Ma than I was nervous of the weekend therapy with her and another girl's family. I found it quite interesting seeing the way they interacted and how their family was around each other. It was more fun than a normal day there, anyway.

Ma looked sad and was quite quiet, obviously finding it difficult to come into this strange environment and bare her soul.

There were a lot of diagrams on a white board and explanations of an addict's journey. But nothing about the addict's mind which I find the most valuable thing to learn about myself.

How the disease of addiction centres there so it tells me I don't have it.

The thing that touched me the most was a drawing Ma did of our life at the time, with a sad grey house and clouds over the top. How had things gotten so unhappy? That's when I realised how much it had affected her. I really hadn't taken it in before then, always thinking I was the only one suffering.

She had also drawn a beautiful colourful house with a happy sunshine beaming down and smoke coming out of the chimney and a path leading up to it, which the first one didn't have. It makes my eyes well with tears even now when I think of it. What I had put her through is so desperately sad. I just wanted to click my fingers and take it all away and make it great, just like that, but at least we were on the right road now.

You see, even though that touched me so deeply and the love for my Ma was so strong, I still used when I left rehab. No one educated me on my mind and how it drove me to drugs, and how I had to do the opposite of what my head said.

I'm not blaming anyone, maybe I just didn't hear it.

Anyway, the weekend came and went and all I really remember is how I just couldn't wait to get out.

A while after, another family weekend was being scheduled. It seemed like every day they tried to persuade me to invite my Pa, so eventually I caved in and thought, *Fine. You will see!* I tried to be optimistic. How much worse could things get, anyway?

I was embarrassed. We weren't as close as Ma and I. I rarely saw him. Ma and I left him when I was eleven years old and months would go by with us not being together.

He hadn't seen me at my worst and so I felt the whole thing came rather out of the blue for him. He knew I liked a drink and a party but so did he, and I seemed to keep rather in control around him as I was always desperately trying to please him.

Sure, we had smoked pot together and been out to clubs and got more than pissed, but nothing too crazy.

I knew he would hate the place, people included. He was 'above it all'.

I had so much anxiety as the weeks drew closer to his weekend. I was mortified at the idea of talking about hard drugs in front of him and for him to sit there as they spoke of addicts and co-dependency. Ugh.

It's all a blur but I remember standing outside with him in private and he said what on earth was I doing here, what was this place Ma had found? He told me my grandmother would have been ashamed and want me out of a miserable place like this. I smiled and agreed and begged him to get me out! What addict still in denial wouldn't, really!

I played the hard done by and said Ma had taken things too far sending me here. That nothing I had been doing was that bad.

In group I could tell it was all going in one ear and out the other, he didn't speak and didn't answer their questions. He would occasionally say something very him and slightly bombastic, which I could tell took the therapists by surprise. When it came to saying what we wanted changing about the other, he said nothing, that everything was fine and I needn't change anything. Bless him. I had always tried to be the perfect daughter, never feeling good enough. You couldn't be too rich nor too thin for my father. Image was everything. Money and skinny jeans, a nice watch and a quick wit and two fingers to the rest. He was invincible. We were here to live fast and die young.

I asked him to stop lying to me and covering up his relationships with young girls that I knew about.

I couldn't look at him in the eye and longed for the day to be over.

We hugged at the end with me pretending the whole thing was a big misunderstanding and huge drama for nothing, that Ma had set up.

The next day I awaited the therapist's diagnosis of the whole thing. I was soon to be let out and was worried they were going to tell me I had to stay longer. Instead, to my slight amusement and astonishment they asked me if my father was on drugs and that they wanted to admit him as a patient. I guffawed and said that there was no way in hell he would ever admit himself.

He took sleeping pills at night and drank most days but not until drunk – just a couple of beers or a glass or two of wine.

I was surprised then that they could see that in him. I think I was blinded by my own level of intoxication!

He was the master of control, my Pa. He controlled his food and was very slim and young-looking for his age. He had a couple of drinks every night at 6 p.m. to take the edge off and sleepers to sleep. That was how he did life. I can't imagine how he would be if you took that away.

Well I can. A hot mess of anger and frustration. Like a dry drunk, I would guess.

How did he become this way?

A strict upbringing from his father and doted on by all the females in his life? Pa definitely had all the hang ups that he passed on to me. Had he not been good enough for his father? Had he been made feel less than, like he did everyone else?

Is it past life karma?

Had he been spoiled materially and been allowed to manipulate from such a young age it was second nature?

He used to get so angry at many things. With age he has mellowed but some things do baffle me, like the way he gets so disturbed by fat people. Let's rephrase that... why he lets himself get disturbed!

He visibly gets angry at having to even look at them, or "ugly" people. I try to get him to see that the only person bothered by them was him, couldn't he see that he was letting these people he hated affect his life in such a negative way?

What was the point!

Giving people the power to ruin your day just because of how they looked!

I feel bad writing this. I love my Pa with all my heart even through all the past pain and feel disloyal speaking of him this way but if we can perhaps help at least one person to not let things affect them like this then that would be worthwhile. He has such a kind sweet side which makes it all the more hard and sad, as you don't want to be mean about his meanness!

We are so blessed and lucky to have everything one could wish for – material possessions, our health and family – yet mentally, we are a little nuts.

It's such a massive lesson to be able to live in the present moment. To be awake. To have self-awareness. To be grateful. I really see that now.

I hate blaming Pa for how things were but sometimes I found it hard not to. He was away for months of the year every year whilst I was young and when he was there, we had to keep away from him and stay quiet so as not to anger him. Sometimes I see rowdy kids and I can't fathom it. Why can't they keep quiet like I had to?

Every criticism of others that Pa verbalised I took onto myself. That's obviously how he wants me not to be.

Every disgusted look and annoyed glance shot through me. So many ruined meals, upset broken up holidays and occasions by his high standards and hatred.

I saw how strict he was with his diet and it annoyed him that others couldn't have his control. But what life is it to be that consumed with appearance and regime that you lose your own contentment? Is that the thin line of narcissism? And although I see it all in him and dislike it, I feel it all within myself. Subconsciously, that is how I have been wired by him.

Nothing good enough. Not thin enough, pretty enough, tidy enough, not eloquent enough. An embarrassment.

It is why I have such a hard time opening up to people and making friends or trusting. My terror of being judged the way I have been taught to judge. By that impossibly painful high standard.

A lot of my childhood memories aren't happy; why is it you remember the bad more than the good?

Sometimes all I can remember are a series of unhappy meals. Pa would drink wine on an empty stomach and get to the dinner table as if on a tightrope of emotional instability. He would bite his cheek or crack his leg on the table and that would be game over.

I remember his violence to Ma. I remember him hitting her, I remember being left alone at the table a lot. Ma crying in her room.

At night in the dark I feared for our lives.

I lived in my head and had a lot of imaginary friends and animals that would take me to another world.

I never felt I belonged in this one and I didn't want to be here.

Writing this has helped me see even more what happened to us.

We left when I was just eleven. It was a relief. I remember feeling excited as Ma and I roared away in the car. No more anxious angry torment.

I had always been intrigued by drinking and smoking. I remembered my parents' glamorous parties, the ladies sipping champagne and red wine, a cigarette between their long, manicured fingers, tossing their hair back laughing elegantly. I used to come down the morning after parties and drink the last drops out of their glasses and suck air through the lipstick marked fag butts. How glamorous! *I can't wait to grow up and be just like them* I would think, putting my hands through my hair, cigarette butt in my fingers practicing.

As soon as I got to boarding school I got in with the smokers. I was shy and so self aware.

By thirteen I was drinking and smoking daily, and at times getting blackout drunk with my old school friends when returning home for the holidays.

We were all doing it. By fourteen we were smoking hash and having sex. We would steal bottles from our parents and drink in the woods nearby. Vodka, Malibu was a favourite for me and my best friend Kelly. Peach Schnapps, sloe gin... whatever we could get our hands on and was closest to our thieving hands!

I felt part of and finally comfortable in my skin. The awkwardness that I had was slipping away and a new confidence became me.

We were invincible.

By the time I was seventeen and at day college in Dublin I was using every day. Coke, pills, MDMA, skunk, Xanax to get to sleep and stop the anxiety. I hated being alone, needing my gang of friends around me. I smoked skunk from the moment I woke until the moment I passed out. I WAS "FREE".

These were some of the happiest days of my using life. No responsibilities, no one to answer to. No anger, no anxiety. No thoughts. Just fun and controlled oblivion.

I was the girl who hung out with a group of boys. I was never happier.

After scraping through college I went travelling and working through Thailand and Australia.

I never wanted to come home. I missed Ma at times but that was all. I couldn't get far enough away from my past.

Escape.

I returned finally four years later, tail between my legs, after being fired a series of times in Aus and for some of the most embarrassing drunk moments to date. I was smashing my head off plant pots at roof bars and eating the pavement three times a week. They weren't into many uppers where I was so my drinking had become uncontrollable, as did my behaviour.

I felt people were beginning to laugh at me, I couldn't bear the shame. I had to stay out of my mind to cope.

I had several boyfriends, all who assumed we were exclusive and I was going between them all. Lying, cheating, stealing and getting high. I couldn't bear to be sober, even for a minute. Alcohol bored me and I needed my drugs.

Back in the city with coke, pills and everything else, I could control my behaviour more. Keep my reputation as intact as possible.

I got a job dancing at music festivals and toured around Ibiza and some UK dance festivals. "FREE AGAIN".

Always surrounded by people who did what I did,made me feel better.

We would all end up in bed together taking drugs. This was where I felt highest.

Heaven. London was the next stop.

We took a lot of acid and ketamine, smoked opium and other things.

Two of the boys in this group are no longer as they were. They are mentally damaged. They bent the paper clip too far to spring back.

Their poor families.

Two others have died, one to suicide, the other a car crash.

Three of us are in recovery, and the others are still at it.

Since being in recovery I have known four my age die from suicide or using-related accidents and countless other acquaintances I hear of.

My using ended up excluding me even from my heavy using friends in London after a few years. The fun had long gone. Alone, using to live. I couldn't connect with people anymore, other than to just exist and use. I wasn´t in touch with any family and never answered the phone. My spark had gone. Weak, desperate and alone, living in my basement hell.

I was dealing to get by – terribly, as I took most of my stash and my only friend was another dealer who would come over to use with me. She had false teeth and for some reason would remove them when we were really high. I remember scrambling around on the floor with her trying to find them at the end of night… I never knew if it was because she didn't want to leave or she was just out of her mind.

Those mornings when the birds were cheaping and cracks of light peaked through the curtains to say the day was breaking… I would feel suicidal with the dread and fear of not getting to that oblivion, sobering up to the soul destroying thought of having to get through another day feeding the addict.

15. Meath's Birthday surprise

Somehow, I was being let out for my birthday.

I was even being allowed to shack up in a house Ma was renting out nearby with my boyfriend. They trusted me.

Strange!

One of the the first things I did was score some hash and buy wine. We didn't get wrecked, we just smoked and drank. My boyfriend didn't want to as he must have promised everyone to watch over me and have a sober weekend. I honestly can't remember much, other than feeling down, depressed and moody. Still obsessing about drugs and my old life.

I wanted to steal little bits of it back by smoking a joint, rebelling, numbing the darkness but it didn't last long.

I didn't know how to be with him anymore without using.

When I went back in they drugs tested me and I came up clean somehow. I was nervous of being in trouble, even though I wanted to get out I had become used to it there. I had befriended the driver to the meetings and my other peers in the centre. I felt part of. Even if it was just a half life, watching X Factor, something I wouldn't have been seen dead doing before. I started enjoying it, the others seemed to as well. We smoked cigs and drank endless cups of tea and coffee. I'd even befriended a few of the younger staff.

At the meetings I was mainly on the look out for boys! There was one I had my eye on, a hippy surfer with long blonde hair that I found dreamy. I felt like a young teenager at twenty-six. I couldn't speak to him and lost my words when he was about, never feeling good enough for someone that good looking.

I was always cautious who I gave my heart to, I think I was protecting myself from any man ever hurting me again.

I ended up going for a guy who was mad on recovery! Ben.

Bizarrely enough. I think that was a Higher Power working in my life. Thank you!

The Centre let Ben come and visit me.

He was easy to get on with and already had three years clean and sober time. We shared a lot of similar history and using experience which bonded us, and our love for music festivals and party drugs kept us chatting.

Everyone was dead against the relationship, unbeknownst to me.

'Leave that girl alone, the elders in AA would tell him.' Obviously, neither of us listened.

Recovery became the new thing I did with my new boyfriend. The heartache about my lost so-called life of drugs, which still haunted me, did not help, especially at night. I would lie awake for hours crying over that drug and my lost friends.

I saw why I had to lose them though, there wasn't a lot more to our friendship than getting off our faces. I argued there was and yes, we had history and amazing shared memories but they were all to do with getting high.

16. Lizbeth's Christmas

Meath had been in 'there' for two and a half months now and Christmas Day was approaching.

I asked if she could come out and stay out? No, she must stay the allotted three months but did I want to join them all for Christmas lunch? My stomach fell.

Finally, Meath and I persuaded them to allow her out to have Christmas Day and lunch with me at home. The thought of trying to have a happy Christmas just didn't visualise well in a rehab!

We were both quite quiet. I was full of trying to have a happy Christmas but inside I was a nervous jumble.

Unsure of what to say, this was a very different Christmas Day. There were no celebration glasses of wine, as before. I had decorated a tree and there were a few small Christmas presents.

We walked the dogs, a happy normal moment.

I had cooked all Meath's favourite food, trying to make it as happy as possible.

It was a strain for us both. Apart but together, very difficult.

I think we enjoyed our lunch, I think one of us put on the television, probably to ease the silent nervousness of what to say. We couldn't just chat about what's been going on each other's lives, past, present or future.

Just as we were finishing, her father rang with his merry Christmas wishes. She carried the portable phone outside.

It was just a short chat then she came back in, hung up the phone quickly and hurried upstairs.

Lunch ended up down the loo.

He had a strange effect on her, of course, he was unaware how upset he could make her.

I was so upset, not for the food but for Meath and yes, for me, as usual I'd tried so hard and in five minutes, he could spoil everything.

I was sad, frustrated, angry and very fed up.

I drove Meath back and she walked in quietly, accepting her next few weeks left. Both sad and alone in our own world.

17. Lizbeth nervous of Meath coming home

So, at last, Meath would be coming home in a few days.

I was terrified.

I almost didn't want her to be home. I had to be responsible. I didn't feel able.

Life felt very unsafe, unknown.

I talked to Neelam, I needed advice.

Doubts loomed up inside, at least when she was being cared for in the clinic I could indulge myself in solitude, hiding from the world, but my world was coming back and I had to stand up and be ready.

I got lots of advice... never to have a drink! My now much-needed fag and glass or two watching the sunset would be gone.

Okay. I will do that.

I must not fuss, I must not ask where, when, what she was up to. I must shut up and get on with a life. My life. But what life... and allow Meath to get on with hers.

I had to stick to my promise at that family weekend, not to ring her when she was out and to trust in her.

My dear God how, where could I find this trust?

The fear was here now in the front of my mind, what if... What would I do if Meath relapsed? Would I be strong enough to get her back to the rehab? Would we have more arguments?

I so wished for a bit of peace. I wanted to run and hide.

18. Meath's 1st sober Christmas

It was nearly Christmas and the Centre invited Ma to come and dine with us. Somehow we wangled them to let me go home for the day. It was all very alien. Our fun time life felt miles away, everything was serious now, mistrustful and full of unanswered questions. I think I was seen as a ticking time bomb.

It was one of the saddest Christmases we ever had.

I remember being consumed with my eating disorder in order to distract the addict inside from not having a drink or drug...

There was not much joy in anything, as it had been for a while, living with that state of mind.

Everything was an effort and a fight and I felt a lot of things, empty, confused and uncomfortable. Needing something you cannot have so badly. I did not know how to live without a crutch.

I was not ready to surrender and plagued with thoughts of using and euphoric recall of the good times past.

19. Meath Leaving rehab & First relapse

When I was finally let out, I was so relieved and definitely not in a good state of mind. They told me I needed more treatment but as usual I needed to do things my way. I had served my three months.

What happened next is Higher Power work! I got out and near immediately rebelled against the chains of being locked up for three months.

I had heard about a drug you can get at the chemist where if you take over 30 of these pills It gives the effect of DMT. I snorted the lot and ended up haemorrhaging my nose and eye. I couldn't see out of my left eye for two days and the hospital staff told me I could have died if the haemorrhage had happened an inch back from where it was. I didn't flinch, my only thought was I would just swallow the pills in future. And that is what I did the following day. Resulting in projectile vomiting. All worthwhile to feel comatose for a few hours.

Looking back at this in hindsight is alarming. I cannot connect to the hopeless desperate thing I had become.

Quickly needing something better I arranged a weekend back in Dublin to see my old boyfriend that I hadn't broken off with yet. As soon as I was there I scored and we went to a club. It was strange being with everyone. I could tell they were wary of me, not wanting to be the ones to be blamed for using with me or influencing me. It wasn't the same.

I yearned for the old high.

The old times of fun with them and no responsibilities. I was jealous of their freedom. To be able to work and live and just use on the weekends. I was never able to achieve that balance.

I went home with the guy who had been waiting for me and we got high for forty-eight hours.

Ahhh bliss. Horrible secret, hidden, dirty bliss.

Mind disconnect. Feelings disconnect. What I had been dreaming of for so long.

It wasn't the same in the more lucid moments but it was good nonetheless.

I spoke to Ben at some point thinking I was sober enough but he couldn't understand me. He was coming back to the station to pick me up later that night.

I rolled off the train drunk and high. He told me he finally realised the worry and concern he must have put his parents through. But I selfishly didn't care about his feelings in that moment. The beast was alive.

I went through a series of those type of weekends. Being with Ben in the week, going to meetings and then having blowouts at the weekend. I had stopped even bothering to contact my old friends – I would just go to the city to score and then come home and secretly use. Adrenaline, my old friend, pumping through my veins. The anticipation of picking up in the city would carry me through the weekdays when I had run out.

The last weekend I returned from I remember sitting on the train in total fear. I had a bag full of drugs – enough for a week in Ibiza for a party of five – but all I could think was what I was going to do when it ran out. My consumption was sky high again and I was back in that place when it had stopped working. My money was near zero, having pawned most of my possessions from Ma's place.

I was back in a place of doom with not many choices.

I looked out of the window as the countryside zoomed by. Suddenly it hit me! This was never going to change!

There weren't enough drugs in the world to stop me! I would never ever be fulfilled.

I could see my life in the coming years consisting of never-ending using and misery and that ultimately, I would die in the pursuit of drugs and feeding this demon inside me.

The saying one 'too many and a thousand never enough' hit me. There would never be enough. I was going to die.

'But I don't want to die,' a little voice said!

I couldn't carry on this way.

I thought of the meetings and everything I had heard and learned. I knew what I had to do.

I used for another five days, sure that this was the end now.

When the drugs ran out, I found a sponsor – the most seriously dedicated to AA looking woman in the room. Someone I knew I would respect and not mess around.

Coming off the drugs this time was rough as I was broken, but in a different way. I wasn't wishing for more with my heart, a switch had flicked, I was just done and I wanted to be fixed.

I would show up to my sponsor's house with my eyes to the ground, body turning in on itself. I didn't talk much, I just listened, my head foggy and we got to work on the steps. I didn't need to talk, I just needed to identify my alcoholism and addiction and keep working the programme and meetings. Everyday.

The first week was murder. The physical allergy craving was crying out for more. I went in ten-minute increments of craving and praying for the obsession to be lifted, calling my sponsor, having a ten minute reprieve and going like that in circles up and down off my knees, praying and crying, gritting my teeth and smoking packets of cigarettes. It seemed like an eternity.

At two weeks clean, I thought I had it licked. I jumped out of bed and, for the first morning since getting clean, I didn't pray, I didn't do my step work or call my sponsor. I went downstairs and opened the mail from that morning to find a wrap of drugs I must have posted to myself from the last use up. I used to do that when I was travelling. I had no recollection of it but I also had no power. Adrenaline surged through me and I ran to the bathroom for a hit... Oh no.

Ugh.

I used all that day and rang my sponsor the next morning.

It was okay, that stuff happens. That's how I learned about my problem.

I was powerless. That morning I was powerless as I hadn't prayed. I hadn't asked for help. I had slipped back into me, me, me and got complacent.

I see how easy it is to relapse especially in the beginning.

The next day I started again fresh and that was the last time I used in nearly 10 years.

Thanks to that power that was helping me, the meetings and the people in them.

It was tough again but with my sponsor, Ben and all the meetings I was attending and other AA's, CA's and NA's I had met that I could ring each day, things seemed to get a little easier.

At six months clean I got my first wow moment. I call it Higher Power but you could call it clarity of mind or being in the present moment, wanting for nothing or God... I had never felt that way before.

It was shivers of happiness that everything was as it was supposed to be and it wasn't because of anything physical, it was all spirit. My soul was finally happy.

It went away, of course, as self got in the way again but I started having those feelings more and more and they spurred me on.

I got a sponsee and showing her the work seemed to give me even more soul food and 'free at last' feelings than ever. I was doing service at five meetings a week, making tea, putting out literature and greeting newcomers as they arrived. This had me coming out of my shell even more and helped me make friends. I would regularly clam up and not know what to say, so service helped keep me busy and helped people to get to know me.

I was still mad but in a good way, a healthier way. My quirky persona was not lost as some of my friends feared. I could tell they thought I wouldn't be fun anymore without drugs.

My eating disorder seemed to take a back seat as well, as the work I was doing was helping me love and forgive myself.

And later, come to accept life on life's terms. That I was born this way, this is my journey, my body, my knobbly knees and they are beautiful as Source, God, or whatever power created them to be. Me shunning myself is really shunning my Creator saying it didn't do a good job.

It's really not about me, it's about us. I started feeling this way the more sober I became and the more I worked on myself. Looking out for others and feeling great from doing so. Finally feeling like I was worthwhile and had purpose.

Instead of spending my days worried about me and my needs, finances etc. I was out there helping people, thinking of others, trying my best at being kind and loving and in doing that, all my needs were met. True inner spirit happiness.

I am now a very grateful addict. (The old me cringes!)

But I cannot deny without being broken, I don't think I would have found this path of light so quickly.

I was suddenly the person that I hated when I was in treatment. I'd never felt so naturally great.

But don't get me wrong, I can still be lazy and certainly not perfect at these practices!

Meath the cynical, sarcastic, selfish, judgemental addict still raises her head every so often and kicks and screams but I have an awareness of it now. I don't have to act on it.

I can ignore her… She likes to isolate and do it alone and fix herself. She can become insular and self-destructive, with negative thought processes. She can be impatient and angry, jealous and fearful, insecure, inflated, egotistical and full of pride! But she's clean and sober and feeling these feelings and living life the way we are here to.

To work through things and learn.

To pick ourselves back up and try again.

To learn love, compassion and understanding.

To let things go.

The negative personality traits happen less and less and are easier to get out of with the tools I have learned and new awareness.

I need unity in my friends, family and most importantly, my friends in recovery who make me realise it's okay to feel and be this way and that there is help.

20. Lizbeth's thoughts of life after rehab...

As I walked my dogs or sat at home I would ponder on the good words and advice I was getting from Neelam.

How to prepare myself when Meath was back home, when life restarts after rehab.

How to strengthen myself, mentally and physically.

I realised I'd always blamed myself when Meath or her father complained or was angry. Tried to make life better for peace and harmony.

I needed to not put up with so much and change myself, protect myself. Stop trying to make life better for others.

It was no use expecting them to change, although I thought if I was kind and patient then they would become more appreciative.

I didn't know then that I was dealing with two obsessive people.

I hadn't known my husband had this obsessive mind and eating disorder, which manifested in disgruntled meals, not wanting to talk about food, not liking too much food on his plate. Obsessing about what we would be eating, or not eating, then not wanting any, or there was too much, or he wanted something else. His thoughts turning somersaults in his mind. I didn't know about this brain chaos. Most meals turning to anger or unhappy moody silences. My indigestion worsening by the month.

In my mind, I'd defended myself as a wife and mother.

Also, my beliefs got me through this, it was a sort of deep personal belief, without talking about religion with anyone. I wasn't the regular church goer, but I just had this strong intuition and conviction.

In rehab and recovery meetings they are asked to believe in a power higher than themselves.

Even for those who don't believe in God surely could believe there is a Higher Power of something that created the world.

I was born and brought up in Ireland, schooled in convents, it was easy for me to pray, believe, hope.

On reflection, I used to think Meath or her father were always trying to push my boundaries, testing my patience until I caved in.

Her behaviour as we got further into her late teenage years had become so similar to her father's. Irritable, snappy, dissatisfied at least with me or her life. We would often have happy fun times together, then the unhappiness would restart.

I'd do a bit more self-blaming.

So it must be me!

If the thought entered my mind that she had a drink or drug problem. I would think it was a phase and soon she would be out of it.

I believe I was scared of losing her, our closeness, to her wild life, to a vast void of the unknown.

21. Lizbeth. Advice on coping with addicts in early recovery ...

Neelam gave me advice for future conversations with Meath and how to cope with difficult situations.

Be interested in what the other person is saying, the power of listening is great.

Share your ideas, only when the person has finished talking.

Don't give advice unless asked, sometimes even when asked it may be better not to give your opinion. If in doubt, do naught.

Don't preach.

When a person is upset, angry, emotional, it's no use trying to be logical.

Give sympathy, company, stay quiet and wait.

Let them know it's okay to be cross, emotional. We are human. We are allowed our feelings.

After the person is calmer, then they can hear good sense and can be understood.

Don't be nosey, stick to the subject which has upset this person.

Don't make light of a serious problem.

Stay calm yourself. One upset person is better than both.

If you are angry, remove yourself physically. Leave the room.

Teach yourself to remove yourself emotionally.

If you can speak, say something like, "I just don't agree" and leave.

I don't have to agree with everything!

I'm allowed to have my opinion.

Agree to disagree, or much better, resume a conversation when you are both calmer.

Give yourself time to think clearly, just refuse to talk until you've cleared your mind.

Stop conversations when you can't take anymore.

So I now learnt to remove myself, unmuddle my thoughts and think clearer, especially if I was tired, upset, too fragile or angry.

We possibly remain tied up in past sentiments, unhappy, and it's hard to move forward, let go, or we'll never be happy in the present.

The knowledge which can be gleaned from the right advisor, preferably someone who has training, is the only correct path to take. Or others one trusts and has actual experience in similar situations.

Listening to some, may be very well-intentioned people, could impede either one's progress.

I found it quite powerful and rewarding to just say, "I can't think now, I'll answer later", and leave the room.

The first time I tried this and it worked, I felt so much better. Hope.

I didn't allow an argument in my bedroom, if possible. I needed this room to be a quiet sanctuary. Eventually I locked my bedroom door, it somehow kept the atmosphere in peace which I so needed. My escape.

If I felt under verbal attack there, I would steer her out and resume the discussion in another room.

I would so easily become upset, take words or looks personally, because of my 'history' of my husband continually blaming me for everything that went wrong in his day or in the home. I was very good at self-blaming and memories of past trauma would exacerbate similar emotions in the present.

I was quite good at hiding problems, pain and angst but then I would be overwhelmed with another despairing emotional trauma and this is what brought me to my downfall.

Sometimes I still felt I had Everest to climb, that I've done so much, tiredness would sweep over me. Neelam suggested writing notes as I went along. More to do. Why did I have to do this 'work'? Change my friends, go to meetings, why couldn't I be left alone in peace, hiding behind the door?

If I wasn't crying, I was angry with the world, angry with this illness, my family's loss. Despair, emptiness.

They say the strong fall the hardest.

Well, I was a positive strong capable person and I'd fallen on solid concrete and seemed to be stuck. I hated it, frustrated if I couldn't stop the tears, angry with myself that I 'couldn't pull myself together'!

I didn't want her to go away to the city! After leaving the clinic, she would try and go and see her friends there, or say she wanted to go to a music festival, promising all sorts,

"I'll be okay, I won't take drugs."

The wrong thing would have been to say an outright "No."

Instead say, "I don't agree."

Meath had to learn how to make the correct decisions for herself. Without my ordering her.

Meath surprised me that first time and didn't go. I was petrified inside, but one other thing I'd learnt was if she was going to use... she could do that anywhere in the world.

So I'd learnt to wait and deal with the problem when and as it happened or I would really make myself more ill than I was already.

If I spent time with any friends and they told me their troubles. I must learn not take on board their upset or unhappiness.

I should try and build up my boundaries, keep an emotional distance.

Boundaries are great at caring for ourselves. I needed to stop giving my all.

Set limits one is able to keep. They bring an emotional or physical 'space' where you don't allow others to cross for self-protection.

In those early days when Meath first came out of the rehab in France I would sometimes feel her tension was at breaking point. I had to resist the urge to say maybe a meeting would be a good idea. I did notice after she went how much calmer she was.

I had no right to, this was her choice to get better. Then I would remind myself from the family weekend if I told her to do something she wanted to do the opposite.

I found a way of thinking and saying to myself. "That's their journey, their learning, their problem," not take any inner emotive feelings into my mind or heart.

The strong reason to this is, we, us Al-Anon lot, get left behind while the clan move on.

They become stronger on their recovery programme, make friends, see a way to live again, live without drugs, work, be happy.

Us lot, we could still be at home, emotionally drained, physically exhausted. Staring out into the wilderness looking for an answer in space.

I also needed to be stronger in case there was a relapse! If there was and I was weak I wouldn't be able to cope if I was still in a fragile state.

So I had to become stronger, learn to switch off my mind and be well and able to cope with the unexpected if it arose.

I would have to let Meath go wherever to see her friends one day. She had to try and take responsibility for herself, give her the chance to choose. No matter how afraid I was.

I had to learn patience and believe in her resolve.

She knew the correct decisions but needs to make them on her own, not my 'telling' her.

She needs to grow, and grow up.

Most importantly, get the reward of making the correct choice.

We must not take that away from them. She must achieve her reward by taking her right decision towards her recovery.

Another hugely important thing to remember we, you and I, us 'Al-Anon' lot, cannot change anyone. Actually, this applies to anyone in life, leave them, the clan member, the choice of changing him/herself for themselves.

We can only change ourselves.

I learnt one way of communicating with Meath instead of saying, do it this way, or don't go there etc.

I would give an example by saying, 'Grandma used to say, to do things this way... or my good friend does this when she feels... or I personally wouldn't like.'

Nothing more. Shut up.

Just give a good example.

Or if there was a particularly difficult conversation or demand, to say, "I would like to have this conversation tomorrow" this diffuses the importance or anger.

Don't TELL them what to do, let them choose.

They have to be in charge of themselves.

When Meath came home, I had to resist the temptation to say, "Get out of bed or look after yourself, or go and look for a job".

At the beginning, without their drug, they haven't the strength to do everyday things. It's a slow process without their 'support' to get through the day.

Give them time, time to realise they 'want to lead a normal life with us' that she wants to be free and well.

Just for today.

I had to trust her big time behind her locked bedroom door, that she wasn't taking anything.

That she did want to live, get up and eat, dress and go out. The simple things we take for granted are a big struggle, especially at the beginning.

We both had so much to learn.

We needed time. As I am an impatient person I had to start with understanding that this could take weeks, months, years. No, actually this stayed with you all your/their life and you had to learn to live with it.

Only you can change you.

Change little by little, one day at a time. It works.

So Meath slowly made friends in the clan group of meetings.

Slowly she didn't need to run away and one by one her friends, the ones she loved, the ones she partied with, the crazy times, were more distant.

But it took years and she realised she couldn't keep talking to them, listening to the stories of their party life and not be there.

This must have been so difficult. This recovery was hard work.

Sometimes I saw that she looked unsettled.

I would wait to see what she might say.

She would tell me that there was a music festival or there was a party she'd been invited to in the UK.

"I won't use, I'd really like to go," she'd announce.

I would say in deep fear, as suggested, "I don't think that's a good idea." Nothing more. Terrified. Then I walked into another room.

I didn't hear any more for a day or so. I would worry inexplicably and suddenly she'd drift into the room and say that she was doing something here in France, that weekend.

I wouldn't react or say anything but inside the relief was enormous. It was like living on the edge of a volcanic mountain cliff and we could both fall off.

Into fire or stay on firm ground.

Gradually and slowly I learnt to go where I felt safe, pace myself, learnt to protect myself, grow stronger and little by little life becomes bearable, becomes manageable, becomes liveable, becomes a more confident world again.

Yes, even a smile again, that there is life, love and can be a lot of happiness.

Just a different happiness, better happiness.

Most of all hope, hope for us both.

At long last the reward, for us both.

22. Meath's world of music festivals

There is a world of drugs and music that go hand in hand and that was my life.

I went to my first music festival when I was fourteen with a girlfriend from school.

Twenty paces through the gates we stumbled upon a tent of cute boys we knew and were smoking hash, giggling and FREE... Like finding oneself or coming home. I was in love, but not with the boys although they were nice to look at. I was in love with the feelings. No rules, no punishments, no judgement, no trying to be what you're not. Freedom. As I stood in a beautiful sunny field listening to the music, the way you get stoned in your first years when it makes the beats of music dance intrinsically through your soul, you become the music, the sunshine, the grass, the smiles, the energy. I lost and found myself that weekend and it started my love affair with parties, festivals and like-minded people. People who lived for the nights, for silent whispers and secret love affairs. For drum and bass and techno. Where people helped you out instead of treading you down.

I never wanted to leave and always had to carry on the party and the feeling outside in the 'real world'.

I chased and lived for that until I was secure in recovery.

It still lives in my heart. A huge piece of it. It still hurts if I go there in my mind. You would think I would have had enough after twelve years partying but it still hurts. I grieved it and after six months to a year, it died down but it's still there inside me. I dream of it some nights and wake up sad but grateful I am alive and well, as so many aren't from my old tribe.

There's not a way that I have found to rave sober (that I enjoy!) but I know many have. I know they have meetings at festivals but that is not me at least not yet. I needed change. Maybe it's because I'm very sensitive and I was so in love with it. Like the boy that got away who broke your heart.

I can't listen to a lot of dance music without it being hand in hand association and euphoric recall with drugs and alcohol.

I can dream of a day I could smoke a joint and feel the vibes but in reality, there is nothing left for me. I smoked so much dope that by the last years it made me horribly paranoid and I always needed drink to calm that. And then you need cigarettes to go with the drink and why not snort some fancy powder to keep you drinking and take a pill to calm the insomnia. It was no longer freedom of choice, recreational using. It was to not feel suicidal.

The drugs don't work anymore.

23. Lizbeth at Al-Anon meetings

At one weekly chat with Neelam, she suggested I try and go to a Coda meeting, which are held at the rehab, for 'us' lot. These were support groups for non-addicts who had a family member or loved one as an addict and took place every Monday evening.

I thought I'd better try, trusting her and her other advice so far.

Off back to rehab the next Monday, I drove. Self-help group meetings, I discovered, were often held in church annex rooms or any other sympathetically-minded centre.

Always hoping for a glimpse of Meath, a quick hug, word of support for me, I wasn't sure which. I didn't find either.

I went to two Monday evenings. I didn't really believe I was a co-dependent. Yes, I suppose my happiness was dependent on when Meath got better, that I would get better.... Is that co-dependent? I suppose it was.

Then I asked myself, was this for me?

The camaraderie was great, their welcome was great. We all said a prayer – a beautiful verse about supporting each other, being positive – held hands, but then each spoke of their weekly troubles with their children or other home or life's difficulties.

I felt more alone. I didn't belong. How would this help me?

I was still far too fragile. I took on their despair in my compassionate mind and became even more upset. I was going backwards into more dark sadness. I couldn't take on their problems, I hadn't sorted mine out yet. Too soon for me to join this group.

Next, Neelam suggested I went to an Al-Anon meeting. She explained these were to help families and friends of addicts. Learn, support, help each other in the understanding of the difficulties living and or loving an addict.

I was screaming inside. More!

Always something more for me to do, go to, learn.

I was trying my best, but was exhausted with trying. Why couldn't I just carry on with my quiet chats with Neelam? I really didn't feel like being out there in the world. I supposed I'd cocooned myself in and thought just our meetings were enough. I didn't feel comfortable with a lot of people spilling their troubles. I thought I'd never do that.

She offered to drive me to the church anteroom where this particular meeting was held weekly. She probably knew I would haven't have gone alone.

We went with one other person who was one of 'us'. Her son was an addict.

Neelam explained to us on the way that each person has a turn to talk only if they so wish about their live life with an addict.

We could get considerable help and learning by listening to each other examples.

Make comparisons and that you were not alone going through this difficult lonely path.

Neelam tried to get me to promise that I'd go to six meetings. I'd try. *What a nightmare*, I thought. I didn't want to go to this one but I did want to do all I could to learn to help Meath and myself.

We, about ten of us, joined hands and said the Serenity Prayer. There was a lovely feeling of belonging with others, with other people who had family or loved ones with various addictions. I didn't speak, I was far too nervous. I just listened.

However, listening to a few young mothers relating stories of their problems with their husbands, car, computer or household difficulties and one woman telling about her home life with her alcoholic husband, I was having difficulty distinguishing this from a coffee morning with a few pals. But there was a different feeling of silent understanding there.

A trust. Total confidentiality. There was a bond. I'd have to go to a few more. I would try and give it a chance.

But I found I could not glean any mental support or learn from their experiences. I felt sadder. There seemed to be so many people around living a life of trouble and sadness.

I gave it a miss for a month.

I had a few more of my chat sessions. Meath seemed to be progressing or at least not fighting the world, me and herself.

So I mustered some courage and went to another meeting, on my own this time.

I had decided I would speak and share some of my therapy knowledge to tell a bit of my story, which is voluntary, and helps one not feel alone with the problem.

As Neelam had explained, one should relate a story example to help another around the table, listen and find the similarities in your life, thereby gaining an understanding of your experience and learning from another's story and example of recovery.

There was no order to who started after the chairperson, there would be quiet, then someone would start. One or two started their usual chat, then a young girl started talking about her mother who had come home and had started drinking again. This girl looked and sounded so sad. She was blaming herself and couldn't comprehend why her mother had started drinking so much again.

I waited until she finished talking, as there was not meant to be any cross-chat conversation.

I started talking, quietly at first, very nervously, keeping my eyes on the wall. I said my daughter was an addict. I said I had learnt it was not hers or any one addict's fault, and if an alcoholic had relapsed, she couldn't help it as she had the disease of addiction and needed help.

The girl chatted back to me. She couldn't believe it. We discussed this very briefly, she looked happier that she was not to blame.

Then, to my surprise, the chairperson suddenly closed down the meeting. They reprimanded us for the cross chat, said the closing words and we all stood up.

I was in shock. I couldn't speak to ask someone to clarify. I looked at the chairperson, at any of them to see if someone could explain what I'd done. I drove home with tears streaming down my face in complete confusion. I was angry and distraught.

Were we not there to relate our story, support one another, give our knowledge?

Okay, we cross chatted for a minute, but I was a newcomer. I had answered the girl when she exclaimed and needed to know if it really wasn't her fault.

This particular bit of knowledge had helped me so much.

I'd believed for years it was my fault my daughter and husband behaved as they did, because I did or didn't do things right for either of them. I felt beaten again.

For this book, and out of respect for other Al-Anon meetings all over the world, I went to a few more to find out how one learnt at such a meeting, in the expectation that I would hear a message, learn from someone.

A year later I attended another meeting in a different town a long drive from home. They were more welcoming, started the meeting with the usual preamble. They welcomed me and I'd brought a friend with me whom I thought would benefit. This friend had just started a relationship with a man who she suspected was an alcoholic and needed some support and information.

There were various people of different ages, quietly spoken, with kind supportive looks.

They welcomed us. Most were French people; my French was just good enough to follow it. They were so open and friendly. As usual starting with the codes and rules of privacy and respect for all in the room.

The chairperson was very serious as she read out all these rules. We joined it at various points, each was given a paper with all the words, rules, and prayers. Various people gave their story of trauma that they wished to unload. Everyone listening quietly, respectfully, understanding the deep anguish inside every person in that room. The pain and compassion visible in their eyes. They stopped after a while and gave out coffee and biscuits. This was a chance to chat and make a connection to a few of them if you wished. Then the meeting continued. I felt hugely better and the lady I brought with me was amazed there seemed to be so many people in this country and world who had similar troubled lives, and that there were these hugely private groups where you were made very welcome. You made a connection, learnt and supported each other.

There is no money involved. It is not run as a business – all voluntary. All over the world for us all.

I have huge respect for them and that they help many, many people in loneliness and despair, thinking they are the only ones going through their personal family hell on earth.

Also, I learnt that some therapists or meetings don't suit certain people but suit others, it's very personal, your problem and your needs. I was glad to have had the opportunity to see the differences in meetings and therapists and certainly grateful to have found my particular therapist and my learning experience for our future.

I had to get to terms with, as crazy as it sounds, this already selfish addict daughter of mine would have to become more selfish, as when on the road to recovery they have to put themselves first. They go to their meetings, talk to their sponsors, read books, do the twelve steps and concentrate on themselves as it is hard work at the beginning. They are also advised after several months to take on a sponsee, a newcomer into the programme of recovery. As I learnt this is part of their learning, to help and give to others.

I learnt to step back and allow her to get on with this.

I remembered once I had to go to a skin specialist and needed an injection in the top of my head. I was nervous and Meath offered to accompany me. *Great*, I thought, I felt better already, but as we were entering the room Meath's mobile rang and of course she answered it. It was her sponsee. She rushed out of the room and stayed talking to her sponsee the whole time, even as we walked back to the car. I felt hurt, unsupported, unloved and very sorry for myself. More tears, and then anger at myself.

Meath seemed to be aware of my upset, after her hour-long conversation, said she just had to help this person right away, as she needed to stop her sponsee from relapsing. There was definitely no, 'Hang on, I'll call you back' attitude.

More of my learning, not to expect.

After all, I am not a trained therapist nor do I fully understand.

I must be patient, I must stand back, give her space to grow.

Resist the temptation to put my bit of advice in.

Trust in the rehab, trust in the meetings and trust in her.

I must just be there when she comes out, to give her love, a roof and food but step back and let her learn her way to recovery. Only wait if and only if she might ask me for advice, otherwise I must shut up. I couldn't help any more than that.

Meath can't help me or anyone until she's helped herself.

If you want your loved one to have as normal a life as possible, give them time and freedom to recover, let them be selfish to mend. Then we can all benefit.

I knew my daughter was the kindest, loving and considerate girl, but addiction had grown and grown and now the angry addict side of her character was winning over the beauty.

Lastly and most importantly, she must get the reward of her being able to succeed alone, away from me.

Her choice.

Her work to learn.

Even for the one day.

Even just to the next meeting, just the next step.

HER reward.

The power of talking. For us both but not together.

I was learning. Through Neelam, I was opening up, getting rid of all this pent-up stress, hidden angst, ignorance. I was unloading and it was beginning to work, slowly. Things were feeling better.

It stops the mind racing. Stops the obsessing.

Clears the brain.

Talking with someone who has a similar experience and lived through a trauma as you. An understanding listener.

24. Meath explains meetings to her ma

It's best to try quite a few different meetings in order to find where you fit.

I hear of people rejecting recovery, saying it's too Bible- bashing or religious. I haven't found this at all but I have heard some meetings have people who are very religious in them so when they then speak of God it may seem that way, but I would just try a different meeting or a different area in this case.

I've been to some meetings where they only talk of the problem and ego trip how bad they are and what escapades they have got up, one-upping each other. Without sponsorship. I ran from this meeting!

Don't give up on it. There is magic to be found if you can lay aside your initial thoughts and pride.

There's a saying to stick with the winners, but if there are no winners in the meetings, who don't know what they suffer from, then either stay and enlighten them if you are well, or run, if not!

If they don't read the Big Book of Alcoholics Anonymous and it just sits as a door stopper at the exit, then they don't know what's wrong with them, or their family. It's more of a support chat group. Full, most probably of victimhood and blame...

Which will not get you well! We have done enough of that in our using/enabling lives!

Whether you be Al-Anon or AA, the addict or the affected family member.

I have to say, 98% of the meetings I've been to over the years have been great... So welcoming and supportive, compassionate, funny and full of wisdom, strength and knowledge. Acceptance and gratitude.

We are blessed to have each other.

When we are well, we can laugh at our dark side, we have camaraderie and a huge connection.

My new friends are all ages, from all walks of life. I could never have imagined connecting with such a variety of truly lovely big-hearted people, all joined with mutual understanding of our similar experiences.

25. Lizbeth. Ben the boyfriend moved in...

So Ben was about to move in, was I mad, but it seemed better than Meath moving out.

Neelam also advised this relationship might help Meath learn more and she would have someone to go to meetings with.

She was just back in my life, this new way of life. I felt nervous and worried but then wasn't this a normal part of my life.

We rearranged the house a bit, so upstairs they could have a small sitting room and kitchenette by their bedroom. We could be separate but all have more privacy. I hoped this would work.

Ben and I were a bit wary of each other, we'd met a few times, he seemed nice enough, was polite, a bit reserved, but for Meath's sake I believed we would all make it successful.

Always the hopeful one.

Ben couldn't really afford a place for them both and Meath, for now, wanted to stay at home.

I'd had loads of input from Neelam.

I must make them both contribute to food, utilities and jobs around the house. If we had a problem around the practicalities of running the house, or anything, we were to sit down and have a meeting, us three!

Meetings like they did in their rooms!

I was not comfortable being like a housemistress. I'd been the rebel at school, this role didn't sit well with me.

Ben had other jobs to go to most days. He said he'd worked in lots of various odd jobs. He didn't have enough work and wanted to earn more, from me or he asked whether I knew of any friends who would give him work. Maybe I could find a few jobs here? Perhaps this could help us both.

He arrived.

Meath knew where lots of meetings were now. Ben knew of more and they seem to get into their way of life quite quickly.

The first few weeks passed easily enough. I could hear them in the distance chatting away upstairs, often laughing, which was lovely to hear again. They seemed to get on well. They'd go off to meetings together, write lots, talk and seemed happy.

It was good for Meath to have company, a boyfriend I could see was helping and someone who knew so much about addiction.

I continued my visits to Neelam, they were getting less frequent now. I wasn't yet partying but could go out and chat in small amounts. I would test myself and try to increase my confidence in the world again and myself. I loved gardening design and found a neighbour who wanted their garden redoing so I immersed myself in this work. It was perfect for me I could work by myself and as hard as I liked which helped me cleanse myself of worries and stresses. I relaxed in nature and creativity.

As the weeks went by, I started noticing Ben's black looks when he came home from work sometimes. I'd smile and call out 'Hi'. To receive no answer.

I would let it go, but after several weeks I mentioned it to Meath. She looked uncomfortable and said 'Well, don't speak to him or look at him when he comes back.'

Then I found if I was in the garden when he came back from one of his jobs, he would glare at me or I could see his silent stern face.

I supposed he was tired and would make up excuses for him in my head.

But I could not help think, 'Where's the harm in an acknowledgment wave, a smile?'

When I asked Meath about him seeming unhappy or angry, she would say, 'Just ignore him, he'll have had a bad day.'

It got to the stage if I thought he'd be returning I would make sure I was somewhere else in the house or garden.

This is crazy, I thought several times. I hid my irritation as best I could.

More time passed and Meath said Ben knew lots about his building knowledge. I could tell he wanted more work, money and she wanted him to be happy.

I made a list and on Meath's advice, I agreed an hourly price and gave him a few odd jobs. But silly me, I thought he would discuss a few details before he started but he didn't. He crashed on in his own way and when I saw several things I wasn't happy with I confronted him in a friendly manner, to see his blank stare back at me, as if I was the female idiot who knew nothing. I supposed I should have talked to him but having any conversation with Ben was becoming strained. He just thought he knew best.

I felt his annoyance. He silently and tensely carried on.

His anger was visible, he sighed repeatedly. I mentally sighed.

I realised he didn't want me near him, and like a spoilt child, he only wanted to do it his way.

I suppose the resentment with each other had started with us both quite soon.

He wanted the control, maybe he wanted to be man of the house.

He'd asked me for the work and I was paying.

Meath chatted to me later, as she saw both our irritation. She explained that Ben felt he knew where or what to do and preferred to work on his own. It seemed so trivial and ridiculous. I mentally defended myself that this was my home and my job and I was paying him!

Gradually as the weeks went by, I felt his resentment of my being there at all.

I wanted to be sure how he did whatever job the way I wanted. I had renovated seven houses and redesigned several gardens so felt confident in my knowledge, plus I needed my personal choices. I was qualifying my own reason for being in my home and for the jobs! Why was my opinion being dismissed? My confidence was shaky enough, perhaps I should back off and let him for Meath's sake?

More inner turmoil.

Meath said perhaps it would be best for him not to do any work for me, just for other people. That was fine with me. I had worked side by side with my builders in Ireland for years, discussing, organising the work together.

I was defending myself, my feelings and actions, again.

Confused and irritated I kept quiet.

When things got too difficult Meath suggested a meeting, yet again.

They took these seriously. I had to learn they might help.

We chatted about little things, cutting the grass if he could do this weekly, like we had agreed at the beginning. I found these two quite relaxed in these chats, they were used to them. I wasn't, at least not like this.

We'd sit at the kitchen table and each have our say. I remember at one I reminded him about the grass cutting, as we'd agreed that was one of his contributions to living at our home. He cut it the next day, I thanked him and said how good it looked. "I liked it better before," he replied gruffly.

At the end of our chats, we'd apologise and hug. The first time it made me feel hopeful, then after several of these, by now weekly chats, I didn't feel so hopeful.

Sometimes they asked for a meeting, occasionally I'd ask for one.

But I was beginning to not have much belief in the so-called apologies.

It seemed insincere, like going to Confession and then committing the same sin again the next week and it was becoming impossible to just casually ask him anything.

I was by now uncomfortable and unrelaxed in my own home – my sanctuary I used to call it. There was definitely no longer any harmony. I was being as patient and considerate as possible but getting little in return.

What was happening? How could this be resolved?

I went out more, walked the dogs more, hid in my room watching TV.

I questioned myself, my behaviour, I was trying to stop blaming myself, I justified my feelings.

I didn't demand, I tried to stay out of their way, give lots of privacy, cook meals which Meath could collect and they'd eat together. I didn't ask for their company.

I told Meath not to worry about me, I was fine. My priority was that she was stronger in her recovery.

But was this acceptable?

Was this tolerable?

Was it wrong of me the ask for the paid work to consider my wishes and opinions?

I didn't want any more insincere home meetings, they got us nowhere. It seemed to make them feel better but I definitely didn't believe in them anymore.

I would hear him say sorry. I would accept it, then I seemed to see him walk off as if he'd got away with it again. I'd put a stop to the hugging, his were definitely insincere.

So my resentment steadily grew. My inner anger at myself increased for trying to help their life and I suppose I at least expected some sort of an appreciative good feeling in our home.

I was having this strong déjà-vu feeling of my married life.

Nervousness at home, unsure of the reception I would see whenever my husband came home, banging doors, pent-up anger. I recognised all the signs.

So more self-examination, maybe it was me and how I am.

It must be my fault.

My ex, my daughter, and now this boyfriend, behaving the same way towards me.

I realised Meath was in a difficult position, wanting to get on with me and wanting her boyfriend.

I reminded myself he was helping her learn about so much about recovery. They would read and study the Big Book and do the twelve steps repeatedly.

Months passed and I would notice Meath coming to be with me, and then skuttle back to see Ben, with a deep worried look on her face.

She was trying to be the middle ground diplomate.

The strain was telling on us all.

History was making me feel bullied and fearful of his anger.

He wanted control, just like my ex, and achieved it with anger.

I'd hear him chatting away happily on his mobile for ages, especially when he was meant to be doing a job for me, hourly rate, and then he'd see me and of course, glare. I'd say nothing. Always keeping the peace. I wasn't peaceful inside. If I'd make suggestions, he'd contradict everything.

I talked it through with Meath – no more Ben jobs.

How much more could I cope with? Was he hoping I'd move out?

The stupid thing was we were both pandering to him for the peaceful life. Just like life with my ex.

It was a horrible, horrible feeling that someone close to my daughter resented me being in her life and resented my being in my own home.

Living together was making me so sad and I hurt. I could also see that Meath was hurting.

I remembered some therapy words, 'No one has the power to irritate you unless you allow it'

I was allowing this life but couldn't stop it.

I had to find the strength to get back control of me, my life, my home, my feelings. I'd done this once with my ex and was now doing it again. When would there ever be peace?

At one point Meath went away for a night.

Ben returned home from his work and he had decided to make another so-called amends meeting with me.

I was working in our garden, in my peaceful place and felt as he approached that I didn't want him intruding in my private space. The three of us had already had a tense week.

He started by the usual, "I would like to talk, say I'm sorry..."

I exploded. I threw down the spade and turned on him,

"Don't come and say endless sorrys and not mean them. I don't want to hear them anymore." I shouted back at him. I was so angry.

He stormed off shouting back at me.

The peaceful atmosphere shattered. I'd had enough.

The image and atmosphere of our argument stayed with me for a long time.

Later on that evening, I heard doors banging over and over. Getting louder and louder, I thought they would break. I heard the loo flushing, over and over, water running, doors banging.

I went to my bedroom and locked the door.

I didn't feel he would be violent to me but memories of my ex came back.

I felt frightened, then angry, this was my home, my peace. I didn't want to live like this anymore.

I was living in my home where I was not wanted.

History repeating itself.

I'd lived in my husband's home, and he'd always called it, 'mine, mine, mine'.

But now I'd managed to get myself into this hopeless ridiculous situation, again, trying and wishing to help and be kind but above all, be close to Meath and for her happiness. Most of all, her recovery.

I was now angry. At myself. At the situation. When would I learn?

Oh, stupid me, I thought.

I needed help. Again.

Neelam had helped me get stronger but I could feel myself sliding backwards very, very quickly that night.

I hardly slept. I kept listening out to see if he'd come anywhere near my door.

I wanted him to move out. Ben didn't want to move out. Instinctively, I thought *He wants me to move out*.

I didn't know how to confront him personally.

But I was beginning to change as I asked Meath to suggest what on earth we were to do as we/I couldn't live like this anymore.

Meath went to see a different therapist occasionally, now she was out of rehab. She had been recommended to a lady who continued to help her weekly.

So Meath told her about our problem. She, Amanda, suggested the three of us come and talk it all out with her!

Great, I thought. *Some help at last.* Then fear and worry. Maybe she'd tell me it's all my fault. I began to think she'd say I must be more understanding and reasonable.

This was a ridiculous situation, having to need someone to adjudicate between us. More muddled thoughts whizzed through my tired mind.

We made the appointment.

Meath and I drove together.

Ben arrived on his own.

I was extremely nervous. I couldn't imagine how she would cope with us. What would she say to us?

We sat down in a circle. Amanda said we would all have our turn to speak and say what we saw as our side of the problem and situation.

Amanda asked me to start.

I drew breath, feeling sick and stressed. I felt flushed and hot.

Why did I have to do this? More, more of me.

I had made a few notes and tried to relate my side in an as unemotional, factual way as possible. Trying to pretend I was talking to space.

I spoke of the resentment I felt towards me when I was in my/our home and the unhappiness of this impossible situation which was becoming worse.

My hope at the start was we could all give space and respect to each independent life but how I felt Ben's anger and irritation towards me.

Meath sat between us not looking at either one of us.

Ben had his eyes shut.

Amanda interrupted me and told Ben to open his eyes.

Apparently, this helped him to not hear my words and reject what I was saying.

I felt very hot and bothered, red in my face and couldn't wait to finish.

I glanced at my notes again to get restarted. I was glad of them as I didn't want to ramble, just say the condensed to-the-point phrases.

I continued, saying that I was upset that Ben had abused my patience and kindness. I was cross with myself for putting up with his rude behaviour for so long. Over a year by now.

I was now interested in my health and my happiness in my home. And I had asked for this meeting so hopefully we could all stay friends and understand each other.

I said I liked Ben as a person and thought he was a good kind man under all his angst but sadly I couldn't cope any longer with his temper and disrespect for Meath, our home or me.

He could visit, stay a night but I no longer wished him to live in our home anymore. Meath could go and stay with him if she wished.

Ben snorted.

I thought and hoped she wouldn't but she was of an age that if that's what she wanted I wouldn't stop her.

I then said I resented having to make this meeting as we couldn't sort things out on our own but found him frightening and difficult to communicate with, not all his fault, it was my past abuse from my husband and that I found his anger brought out similar fears in me.

Meath was next. I heard the pain in her voice.

I hurt also and felt the anger rising against him for this stupid situation.

Meath related her side, how it was so difficult living between two people she cared about.

Going between us both, trying to keep us both happy and it was really hurting her.

She looked tired and pained.

Ben's turn. I tensed. He blamed me for interfering in odd jobs he did for me around the house and I should have given him the cash and a free rein.

I burst out, "But you didn't have the knowledge or experience I have."

My turn to be told to be quiet. I fumed at him.

Finally, Amanda had her turn.

I held my breath. I couldn't imagine how she could sort this out and was positive she would tell me it was my fault. To my amazement, she said at an agreed time in the following weeks it would be a good idea if Ben would move out. It was obvious things at home were too stressful to live happily under all these resentments.

Amanda asked if I would allow him to stay while he found other accommodation. "Of course," I said, "take two or three weeks."

So Ben moved out... the next day.

He must have been so unhappy in this situation. As we all were.

I was so relieved that terrible scene was over and Meath seemed happy and thankful also.

Meath then started commuting between homes.

I coped on the outside but inside I felt upset as I really didn't want her to end up marrying a man who seemed so like her father. Such 'an out of the blue anger' he had.

When I saw her packed bag and knew without asking that she'd be staying with him for a few nights or weeks. I forced myself to say, "Drive safely, have fun."

I was determined to keep her request not to ring and worry.

I trained myself to get on with my life. Not look at the phone or if she rang, not expect the worst.

She would thankfully text. I didn't text first. I had to trust her and give us time.

So it wasn't my fault totally. Thank goodness. In the end, I was very glad we'd gone down this route as no way on earth would we have ever been able to have talked between ourselves about Ben leaving. It would have just gone on and on... false short-lived apologies and more anger.

About a year after Ben moved out, he emailed me to ask if we could meet. He wanted to make amends.

I didn't know what to say or do. I asked Neelam what this amends was all about.

She explained... He will talk and say all the things and ways he believes he has hurt and upset me. I then give the respect of listening and not interrupting or making light of it. He will then ask if there were any other hurts he could have made to me and overlooked and I should say if there were. Then he will ask my forgiveness which I do not have to give.

I thought about his email.

I wasn't ready to do this. I replied maybe in another year or so, he could contact me again.

Everything was far too raw. I couldn't have been honest and listened to something I still felt wouldn't have been honest and true in his heart.

Also, I just didn't feel like forgiving easily anymore.

I was still too new and emotions too sensitive... the hurt too painful... my learning too new. Meath was only still two years in recovery by now. I was only a few notches up from fragile.

Thinking back, I remember being nervous of having a confrontation with Meath or Ben, in case either of them relapsed. I couldn't have taken that self-blame.

My gentler harmonious approach to our living together was as a nervous wreck from the start.

I now know it wouldn't have been my pushing either of them over.

They have to be responsible for themselves and I must behave normally. It would not have been my fault.

I had to 'see' my part in this whole affair. I was too sensitive and nervous of pushing them, had I blown up regularly, or snapped at him or had the strength to just chuck him out earlier. But Meath was new out of rehab and I had a great need to be near her. Not see her all the time, just be around nearby. We were a close mother and daughter, we needed each other's support and love.

I just couldn't lose her to a man I hadn't know for long and only knew as another sullen angry Jekyll and Hyde type. And I knew one of those and what mother doesn't want her child to suffer a life like hers?

As I was just starting to get stronger from my breakdown. I hadn't yet understood the addict's mind. Nor was I really able for it all. At least not two of them at once.

Ben was struggling with work, money, wanting to be with his girlfriend on their own but needed this situation to be with her. How strong were his addiction voices in his head, telling him lies about me, about himself, his life, wanting to destroy it all?

This was making his anger so strong on a daily basis as he fought his demons. He hadn't been into rehab or had the finances to have private therapy, so his fight was a lonely longer road but he was doing it.

Meath and Ben stayed together for about another year. In the end, she made the decision that she wasn't that happy.
Thank goodness that it was her sole decision.
She was getting so strong, independent and most of all, recovering.

He contacted me again another year later. This time I felt stronger, more knowledgeable, more understanding and forgiving.
We sat and had coffee, I listened, quietly, respectfully... I wished him well. Yes, we slightly hugged as we said goodbye. I felt he meant it.
Also, I knew what to do and say this time. Meath had made her amends to me that summer, under a tree in a beautiful garden. Of course I cried, but not from pain that time, from some hope and love for her bravery.

Meath; sometimes the road seems long and unending of darkness… just hold on tight and work hard doing the next right thing, getting stronger day by day, ready for the magic to happen. Taken by Meath when suffering suicidal thoughts and despair.

26. Meath, life with Ben & Ma

Ben and I convinced Ma to do up a house together to bring in some money. These situations should come with warning signs! In hindsight it was mad to think it could ever have worked.

For a man to work under a woman, let alone two women, takes quite a man.

It was really difficult. We all wanted to do things our own way and I spent those few months treading on eggshells around everybody.

I had found myself in another relationship triangle.

It was a huge pull on me, trying to keep everyone happy, and the others to fill their part. I so wanted Ma to be happy with the choice of man I had chosen to date and yet also wanting Ben to be kind and respect her.

Ben's main frustration at the time was not having enough money, but being a typical addict, he didn't want to answer to anybody at work. Especially not his girlfriend and her mother! Things were really tense.

Unconsciously I started acting out in the only way I knew how without drink and drugs and that is to control my food. I cooked for everyone to keep them fed and happy and show my man I cared, in the hope that somehow it might lessen his frustrations. Meanwhile, I barely ate anything. Unhappy, but high on starvation. I started taking it out on Ben's poor cat. She was old and rather smelly but I started really resenting her in the house and hated her in my bedroom. I see now that was deferred anger. I couldn't be angry with Ben or Ma and I was so full of self-hatred and frustration with my situation that subconsciously I had decided to hate the poor cat. She was harmless and sweet and I had never felt harmfully about any animal – on the contrary, I love all animals. But she was setting off my OCD and also blissfully unaware of the pent-up emotions in the house.

My OCD went through the roof and I kept everything insanely tidy and straight. It was the only thing I could control. If things weren't the way I liked I would lose it inside, everything would crumble and I would feel lost and scared.

So I was angry with the cat, tidying like mad and not eating much food…

Being in a starvation state with anorexia or bulimia gives you a high. When I was controlling my food, eating less, knowing I was getting slimmer, it disassociated me from everything else.

Like drugs did. It stopped me thinking of whatever's going on so I can think of me, food and my body. Everything else pales and I would feel lighter with adrenaline and not enough calories.

I don't know why I didn't just kick Ben out there and then. Our arguments had got worse and worse. He didn't hurt me but he let his temper out on everything else. He smashed up the wall outside with my car in one angry temper and told me it was my fault. Mum's fault.

When things were good, they were great. He had a wonderful sense of humour when he wanted to and knew how to make me laugh. I clung to those few and far between moments to keep it together, like the memories of our first Christmas, when we were both unemployed and had no responsibilities and no parents around. It's easy to be happy then. It's when life shows up with demands that you see what's really going on inside a person, I think.

I identify with his pain.

The bigger my life has become with people wanting and expecting things from me, the more difficult it is to remain in a state of calm! Especially as an addict with a mind you need to keep well. This should be our primary focus. Keeping mental health and recovery in check.

It went on in this awkward way for a while until it reached a head. My therapist, who I saw weekly, suggested we do a family therapy meeting. Ben (staunch AA and very anti-therapy) was going to love this! As was Ma, being hugely private and anti-establishment...

Ugh.

It was pretty torturous and it went worse than I thought. Ben just stared at the floor, he was so angry and Ma I felt so sorry for, sat there obviously pained.

We couldn't see any way of solving things, apart from splitting us up, which I have to say I felt that was the right thing to do. I loved Ben but things really weren't right and it was misery.

My fear of being alone and not finding anyone was huge, my irrational fears that have run my life, so sad! I was so young still but terrified of being alone without a man to love me.

I couldn't really talk either, after they both spoke their bit I, surprisingly at my turn, after a long pause of silence, started shouting obscenities at them both! All the months of pent-up frustrations pouring out in a nonsensical flurry.

It was over.

This would test my recovery foundation to the max!

I started getting in touch with people from my past to make amends with, people I had previously harmed to apologise which was part of the 12-step programme. There were a lot of good friends who had been cut out or who had removed themselves from my life due to drugs and my behaviour. I tried to mend bridges with the well ones who had good lives now. I saw it as a bit of a life line, as otherwise the only people I knew were in the AA fellowship.

I had a year being single, for the first time in over 10 years. It went from being really scary to being one of the best things I have ever done. I was doing things that I actually liked! That I wanted to do when I wanted to do them. I had no one to answer to and I was independent. Wow!

I was doing service at every meeting I went to and really stuck to the people who were working hard at their recovery. Which really helped me stay on the straight and narrow.

I worked in a friend's shop in the mornings and started training to be a yoga teacher in the afternoons.

Eventually I had saved up enough money to go to Bali with some girlfriends in recovery. I joined a health and nutrition cooking school and finished my yoga teacher training there.

I returned home a kundalini yoga teacher! Who would have thought!

I had also spent a lot of time looking for Mr Right and fantasising who he might be!

I never gave up on my dreams of a safe happy home and a big family. I wanted to create peace and harmony.

I had changed.

Meath. My happy place, where I go in meditation. Memories of fresh food, curries, coconuts. Never have I felt so well and so free.

By the time I was really happy on my own, I met someone.

He was a friend of a friend and I knew instantly he was the one. It wasn't just lust and infatuation, it was also friendship, kindness and understanding, compassion. We took it slowly and got to know each other. Ma's best advice was not to marry in lust but good standing love, as lust goes away and before it leaves it can blind you from the truth of the person you are with.

I feel blessed to have found love, the kind that grows and you don't want to control.

We now have three children, who have been my biggest healers after the steps. Without the steps I couldn't have been the present mother I am, (mostly!) They have helped me be the best version of myself, they have given me a second childhood.

I am eternally grateful for this gift, happier than I ever thought possible without drugs and the biggest gift of my recovery apart from being sober. I see so easily how I could lose it all if I were to stop the work I do.

I can't forget where I have come from. But I do not dwell in sorrow. Forward on!

Now I go to one or two meetings a week, I have a sponsor and I sponsor people. This is the bare minimum, which is what it has to be right now with young children who I give service to on a 24/7 basis!

It could be so easy to get caught up with the mums who drink or my husband's friends. It seems so long ago – 10 years – yet I know deep inside I am an alcoholic and an addict and will always have this affliction.

That when I put one drink or drug inside me it lights a fire the way I see others around me getting lit. The monster arises, more, more, more. I see relapses all around me in AA and I've never heard anyone say that they relapsed and all went well!

We are mentally and physically different. I see people who had years of sobriety, feeling they are okay now, or people in so much pain from not carrying on the work that they go mad and have no choice, powerless to the drink once more. They pick up and some never make it back.

I know I still have the addict inside laying dormant.

I once tried some CBD (cannabis oil) to help my back pain. It sent me totally nuts. I wanted to be taking it all the time. It was all I could think about and on one occasion sent me down a horrific paranoid mind trip.

Gratitude for my clarity of mind of what I suffer from is a huge gift and one I must hold tight, for it is only I who need know this to stay well.

After my third child stopped breastfeeding, I got post-weaning depression. I had been on a pregnancy and breastfeeding high for a few years, having the three of them very close.

It was like postnatal depression.

It really knocked me and brought up a lot of suppressed anger and insecurities. I started waking with the feeling of doom, not wanting to get out of bed in the mornings and became very insular.

I was working a good recovery programme but with the three kids it was a tough and demanding time. My sponsor suggested I seek outside help. I was very hesitant but after having tried the natural route for six months with herbs and tinctures which hadn't helped, in this instance I caved.

My doctor, who understood addiction, prescribed me Sertraline.

Combined with the meetings, they really helped. I stayed on them for a year until things settled down.

I took the prescribed amount and stayed close to my doctor and sponsor who I am eternally grateful to.

I had gone through a big only natural herb stage which I still believe in, but after my experience I now see how they can work well together hand in hand.

I met a doctor who used natural and prescription medication. He was a revelation and I dream of this becoming a more widespread possibility as there are instances I believe when vitamins, minerals and herbs do the trick and are much more beneficial in the long run and then there are times you really need the man-made modern chemicals!

Please take this as my humble human opinion!

27. Lizbeth – my life surrounded with addicts I'd never noticed before

A good friend who lived a few hours' drive away, asked me over for a holiday break when Meath went away.

I had to stop worrying about what Meath was getting up to, trust in her and our teachings and all the last few months work we'd both done. Get on with my life.

I drove over with our dogs in the old Jeep. He asked me about Meath's life and I decided to confide in him and try and explain an addict's condition. I floundered, with my words getting mixed up. I was very defensive of her and didn't want the usual look of, 'of course she could stop' but he sort of understood. He then told me of his youthful drug-taking antics.

It was good to get away, talk to a normal friendly face, someone I trusted and could relax with.

Then I started to notice at our dinners, I would cook and he'd open the wine, he'd glance at my glass of wine, or glance at how fast the bottle went down. If I poured, I would see him looking to see if he had full measure. He would make any excuse if he thought I'd had more than 2 glasses to open another bottle. Or make excuses, all light-heartedly to have cups of tea strongly laced with whiskey.

The sort of thing I'd never noticed before. He'd chain smoke as well. I was not a critical person and believed others should do as they pleased, somehow though, my eyes had been opened to alcohol, obsessive ways and addiction. Alcohol or drugs hadn't been a problem for me, oh yes, I'd partied a lot, smoked marijuana to sixties music, talked all night on 'mandies' we called them, just for a few years but I was always nervous of stronger drugs. I luckily hadn't had the need. Then I lead a normal life, whatever that is, working in various places in the world, social drinking, smoking for a few years.

James and I had our dinner chats, continuing for hours, and I felt he hadn't quite got the meaning of addiction. Why should he? It had taken me months.

I remembered he hated flying. I said, "Imagine when you arrive at an airport, you are waiting outside having your last few puffs, inside the terminal have several glasses of wine. Your nerves getting stressed, your face redder, wondering if you should or could board that plane. Then while you're flying, all you can think of is that next cigarette, you can't think of anything else during the flight. Yes, you can have a few more drinks but you can't concentrate on a conversation by now. You are in your world of despair, desperate for that next drag, that's an addiction.

Then exaggerate it 10, 20, 1,000 times more – that's addiction, when you can't think of anything else.

All normality of thoughts and actions has flown out the window, while you obsess about having your desperate need."

I saw a small dawning on his furrowed brow. I didn't mention his wine surveillance on his frequently empty glass. It was mentally visible to me that he was thinking about whether he could have another, more. I puzzled, was this more than normal or was I now seeing everything in a different light.

"But that's not the same as Meath's?" he asked.

"No, there are degrees of seriousness of the depth of the addiction, drugs, which drug, cigarettes, alcohol, eating..."

"Eating?" he interrupted.

"Yes, I'd learnt people who are bulimic, or anorexic or over eat, that all they can think about is food – no food, not enough food, what to eat, not eat, not eat in front of anyone in case they think they are fat. Continually looking in a mirror and 'seeing' fat on their body."

James interrupted, "Yes," he said, "I have a friend I golf with and after our game we go out for our usual long lunches. He would order so much food and then hoard the bowls on the table near his plate, hurriedly eating and filling his plate again. I noticed while he ate he needed to order another plate of something, looking at my plate in a frightened manner in case I might have some more. I just thought he was greedy!"

"Well that poor man is obsessing about his food, worrying throughout the meal that there's not enough. It doesn't seem to matter whatever the addiction is, it's the obsession. The mind obsessing about what it thinks it can't have and nothing can get in its way," I answered trying in my mind to sort the understanding to myself, as well as my friend.

"It's the more, more, more." I felt sad.

I think my friend was beginning to understand. I didn't ever mention he may have a slight obsession. It didn't seem it was running his life or health too much.

After all, I wasn't the therapist or preacher.

I'm so glad for my little bit of learning.

Understanding James' friend, instead of laughing at him worriedly eating so much, he now had a bit of understanding and felt a little compassion instead of laughing.

Another time a girlfriend came to stay. She was an artist and said she would love to paint en France for a week or so.

I'd never noticed friends or people's habits before this life, this therapy, this little bit of knowledge.

I looked forward to having a friend from home to stay and I didn't want to talk about Meath or our problems. Just have some good light-hearted company. I hoped.

One night we went to a local bistro for dinner. I'd been quiet, felt a bit tired and she suddenly said, "Why aren't you talking? Why don't you amuse me?" Big shades of my ex flashed through my brain. Then I actually tried to start a conversation. *Stop*, I thought, *I'm not her entertainer!* I could have easily fallen back into trying to please others.

Anyway, why isn't she making more conversation? After all, I'd been busy and she had done nothing most of the day. She suddenly looked to me like a bit of a selfish self-centred friend! I let it go, tried not to be upset.

We got through the meal quietly, her sighing and looking around the room for amusement. Me wondering if there were any kind, peaceful people in the world.

She also chain smoked and laughed if the smoke blew my way and I'd cough. "It would be much simpler if you smoked," she'd chortle.

Her hobby was art and she painted all day, the same canvas, when she had made it what I thought was looking good, she'd wipe it off and start again. All the while puffing away, music on loudly and gulping her wine. She seemed oblivious to me or my feelings. I was glad at first, she was enjoying her holiday but now she was beginning to get on my nerves. She seemed to thrive on a bit of excitement, quick to bore, almost if things were calm and peaceful she needed to rock the boat, needed attention like a child. Full of complaints, she was Mrs. Wonderful. I, after all, had had my fill of chaos in my life, I yearned for trusted calm friends.

She loved contradicting me, if I liked her painting she changed it again. If I said what about driving to visit a pretty village or market place nearby, she'd find fault. There seemed to be no agreeable conversation. If I bumped into a friend, she was quick to criticise them, she spoke negatively of nearly everybody.

My final straw was when I'd gone out and left her in a field, painting. She said she wouldn't be back until late afternoon but she walked back to the house earlier to find I'd locked the doors.

I saw her face on my return, she was sitting on a bench by the house, she was furious.

When I got out of the car, she shouted at me, "How dare you lock me out."

137

I was okay up until then. I intended to be calm and nice, but when she shouted something snapped. I walked over. "I gave you a key," I shouted back. "You also have your mobile, you could have text or rung me and I'd have returned quicker!"

When she saw I wasn't backing down, she turned on the tears. I couldn't believe this mature woman was behaving like a spoilt brat.

"That won't work with me anymore," I said strongly. "I lived with someone who used to do that and I'm not putting up with it anymore."

I felt good inside. I was beginning to get stronger and not be a push over, it felt good.

I smiled to myself. At last.

It was no surprise when she left the next morning. Without a word of thanks. I haven't heard from her since, and do you know, I don't mind. I was glad she left. I was beginning to 'see' the takers in people clearer nowadays. Plus, I had to stop 'giving'.

Once upon a time I would have agonised about thinking that it had totally been my fault but now I felt more confident and I sort of didn't care about whether I saw her again with her silly selfish childish ways.

This time I wasn't going to apologise or accept the blame.

How had I never noticed these people before? I asked myself.

They were life's takers, bullies.

I needed to 'detach' myself emotionally.

I acknowledged I would have to change friends as well as my daughter.

28. Meath's 12-step musings, Nutrition & self-help tips

The Importance of Meetings; To carry a message of hope to the suffering addict. To have unity and fellowship. To belong and recover together. To bond with others who have suffered the same. To know you are not alone. To stay plugged into that which I am, a recovered addict that is not cured but in remission, dependant on certain things.

The Triangle: ▲ UNITY, SERVICE, RECOVERY.

When all the sides of my triangle are in order, I am whole.
If I let one side slip, I am like a three legged chair.
Unstable.

12-step programme:

The twelve steps are not religious but they direct you to a power greater than yourself. Of which you may choose or come to believe in or become at least willing to believe – it needs to be anything that isn't you... For how has relying on your own power been working for you? That judgemental punishing God of your childhood maybe hasn't been working? Has kept you resentful/fearful... Atheist? Shameful? Guilty?

We see we cannot rely on our own power entirely to get better.

Nor any other human power, for that matter.

Could that loving family member ever stop you using for any length or time? Did alcohol/drugs come before everything/everybody else? Deep down at the bottom of every human being is the fundamental idea of God.

How many times have I called out 'Help!' Or 'Just get me out of this and I won't do it again...'

Who am I talking to?

A God made up by human pride, fear and ego as a form of control through 'religion'?

I don't think so. I am calling out to nature. To the stars. The Creator. To LOVE. Unconditional. To consciousness. To source, to everything that is – for I AM.

And inside me I find peace. My body is a temple and through prayer – talking aloud or in my head – I connect to that power. Through prayer I talk to the Higher Power/God/higher self... whatever you choose to call it.

Through meditation I listen. I receive answers.

Sponsors (why it is necessary to continue with recovery)

We can recover from a hopeless state of mind and body (active addiction) but we are never cured... We are still addicts/alcoholics (I still have an allergy to alcohol/drugs – when I start, I can't stop.)

We are in remission... We need to stay plugged in to stay that way.

If I take a drink or drug the person who once drank will drink again the same way. Nothing will have changed, apart from maybe it's worse. Body gets older. Disease/allergy becomes stronger.

The alcoholic that drank once, will drink again if they go back to their old ways and don't maintain an altruistic/spiritual way of life.

If I stop these things: Unity (meetings, fellowship, friendships), Service (sponsoring, carrying a message of hope), Recovery. (sponsoring/helping other addicts alcoholics get better).

My spiritual malady returns, I feel bored, irritable, fearful, a hole in the soul which, after a while, only a drink or drug will solve. Suddenly I will have the cleverest idea in the world! A drink! Surely after all this time I can take one or a couple with impunity. Surely, just this once. A treat for all the hard work over the years. A reward!

My mind cannot recall the hundreds of times this has not been the case. That I have never had 'one' drink/hit/fix/snort/pill. I cannot recall the bad times, only the good – euphoric recall from when it 'worked'. And so starts the merry-go-round. I have no mental control by this point. My mind will make up any lie to justify that fix.

Maybe I can hold it together for a while. Maybe I could do a whole year on self-will. But am I happy? Am I free? Am I acting out in other areas? Men, sex, overeating/undereating, control, anger, abuse, shopping, gambling, porn... There are many ways to substitute addiction and kid ourselves we are doing okay.

Can I sit with myself? Am I in the present moment? Or am I anywhere but?

"Bored."

Nothing good enough… Striving for the unachievable, to set yourself up for a downfall and then comes resentment, bitterness… A list of people you have on your black list, banished from your life.

A slave to my own mind... Selfish wants/needs. Do I love myself? How are my relationships with the closest people in my life? Do I let anyone in? Am I the actor with many masks arranging the show? As long as everyone acts and behaves a certain way then everything will be okay? Am I the king manipulator? Ever kind and gracious to fulfil my needs? Or a bully? Does ego rule my life? What is ego? There are many forms – one person has several characters of ego.

Take a look at yourself. Or better yet, let someone else. You might be able to be happy. No matter what you have done, you deserve love and happiness and another chance at a new way of life.

The work to get well...

Twelve steps. First and foremost.

Meditation, listening to recovery speaker tapes.

Through this it is possible to rebuild your life.

Why not give it a go? What more is there to lose? If you get to step 12 and still want to use... Go ahead!

I had to start off like this. I had too many reservations. And I didn't believe but something had happened to me. I saw I didn't want to die or live in misery anymore. I'm glad I was pushed to act quickly with the steps as I saw how the addict mind works quickly to take you back to old habits.

I said I'd do the twelve steps and if I still wanted to use, I would. The world it has then opened me up to is tremendous!

I needed a sponsor who had a working knowledge of the steps. Who has a sponsor, who sponsors others, who attends regular meetings and works out of the Big Book of Alcoholics Anonymous.

Personally, I believe the Big Book was a gift from God or higher intelligence, written through the people at the time, who were alcoholics themselves.

So many incredible gifts have been given to me especially through the amends process. Settling wrongs, forgiving others... To have relationships with some of my family members I never dreamed could be possible again or comfortable.

Such a huge weight off my shoulders really helps and is never as scary as it seems.

I've owned up for stealing things from shops, people etc, faced being arrested and somehow you get carried through. More often than not it is totally different to what my mind tells me it will be. Some of the most difficult relationships I had are now healed.

Words from my sponsor:
Gratitude is an action!

I'm grateful to have my house so clean it! And take out the rubbish!

I'm grateful to have a loving family so don't treat them like shit!

I'm grateful to be clean and sober so help someone else become so.

In this there is much joy and freedom but it's work in practice and it certainly didn't come naturally.

Giving thanks is the highest form of prayer.

Comparing drugs, drink, smoking, eating disorders, OCD, sex, any addictions:

All can be overcome with 12-step recovery. The principle is the same, it's just the first step which is different (as in whatever you are powerless over).

Many addictions come in pairs or more. Layers of self destructive or unhealthy coping mechanisms.

I thought I was just addicted to drugs but when I put one down another popped up. Food. OCD etc.

All of those things change the way I feel. I can't sit with the way I feel without them. See spiritual malady.

The different seriousness's of addiction:

This is explained in the chapter 'To Wives' in the Big Book. The different levels of alcoholism.

Is it taking over your life? Is it number one? Are you a slave to it? Does food/sex/drugs/drink make the decisions for you in your life? Is everything geared around that?

It is possible to be free!

No one has the power to make me feel anything. It is how I deal with the situation.

Set boundaries to not be spoken to/treated that way.

Then I remove myself immediately. Don't enable them to carry out the action. See AL-ANON, CO-ANON, NARC-ANON.

Am I an enabler?
Am I enabling others to stay in their addiction?
Denial?
Throwing money at it?
Saying it's just a phase…. They will grow out of it.
Ignoring it.

New leaves, new life, new beginnings. The tree of knowledge is broad and unending. To love the things you learn and teach is a gift, on offer to us all.

Taken by Meath at the start of her nutritional journey to health.

Nutrition:
For me, when I put down drugs and drink as I have already said, I started to do strange things with food. I was drinking an abnormal amount of coffee and smoking more

than ever, which is terrible for the nervous system (the last thing I needed in the mental state I arrived into recovery at! But I'm addicted to changing the way I feel so I probably needed to go through that experience).

To remain happy and balanced which, believe it or not, has made me lose weight and stay at a stable and healthy place, meant at first I had to cut out all refined white sugar and white flour. (No white carbohydrates as it turns to sugar in the body.)

Sugar is as highly addictive as cocaine!
And for many is a brilliant mentally numbing, mood altering agent mimicking (in the brain) the same as cocaine, as it induces a pleasure and reward experience.

It is dangerous as it is easy to say it´s harmless, legal and found everywhere. But what do doctors tell cancer patients to refrain from eating first when trying to recover?

I know this is not the same for everyone – I think there are people who are more predisposed to being affected... I also believe it to be a mental problem. I have experienced it myself many times over, as a highly sensitive person, especially since removing cigarettes, alcohol, drugs - including prescription drugs… I can now madly feel when I even have a paracetamol the disconnect which I so loved in active addiction and sugar has been an on and off struggle. Overeaters Anonymous helps many people with this.

I made sure I had three meals a day without snacking, each with a component of each food group.

Breakfast: oats with nuts and fruit, coconut milk.

Lunch: one part meat/tofu/protein, one part brown rice/quinoa/rye bread and two parts vegetable with a piece of fruit for pudding. Or a pudding made with brown whole unrefined flour and stevia/xylitol to sweeten.

I believe sugar addiction is also linked with alcoholism. Years of alcohol abuse (alcohol breaks down in the body as a sugar) can make you addicted to sugar, leaving you craving sweet things when you stop drinking.

This makes you susceptible to Candida in your gut. Creating mucous, lethargy, mood swings and sugar craving.

Stevia is a fantastic plant-based sugar substitute. It doesn't contain additives or any disease-forming chemicals like aspartame (AKA sweet poison, cancer forming – found in most low calorie diet drinks and food.)

This was incredibly hard to do as I have a very sweet tooth! But I was using sugar to change the way I feel and I was overeating and feeling terrible afterwards. I was eating erratically and was mentally all over the place with my emotions – Numb/tearful/angry/elated/high/depressed/low/suicidal thoughts.

After a couple of weeks without, which, like every addictive substance, is the hardest, I started to feel the best I ever have in my life.

I ate avocado with pink salt and olive oil or yoghurt with a tiny bit of salt, which overcame the sugar craving and is healthy. I took chromium from an organic health shop to also combat the cravings and level my blood sugar.

Look at the labels of food you are eating. If you can't pronounce or read the ingredients list or they have numbers on the end, maybe think twice! They can wreak havoc on your body, mentally and physically.

I choose organic food where possible; if eating meat I would choose grass-fed free range where possible. Otherwise, animals are sadly pumped full of hormones and veg is sprayed with pesticides. If they kill bugs then they must be slightly poisonous. If we are eating that every day it is going to build up in our systems and create illness. Do research!

Live kefir is brilliant for rebuilding the gut, which is responsible for our happiness and also immune system.

I love following organic or vegan-minded chefs on social media for inspiration.

Food does not have the nutritional content it once did. Magnesium is a great mineral to use in the early days (it helps you relax), as is a high dose of vitamin C, D& B complex. I was incredibly depleted in every sense and needed the strength especially when I stopped smoking at a year clean, for which I used the programme, prayer and white knuckles. By week three the nicotine beast was gone but what a mental ride to get there. Thankfully it was so horrific I could not go back again no matter how enticing it might be some evenings. (It also helped that smoking had given me a scary claustrophobia when I woke a wheezing mess in the mornings with my first fag… so attractive!)

You can overcome many things with 12-steps and a good diet and added vitamins and minerals! I needed Q10 to help my bloodflow as I would get faint a lot.

I also recommend a food intolerance blood test, this really helped me clear up some mild acne caused by dairy intolerance I was unaware of. Acne is linked to the gut. Emotions are also linked to the gut. Years of anxiety, anguish and drink and drugs on an empty stomach had taken a toll on my system.

I had to heal my gut, with probiotics, no processed foods or sugar etc… which aids the happy vibes as well as making you glow!

You can get online tests sent to you easily and fairly economically. I know this might all sound rather a lot to do but for me by the time I was a few years clean my reasoning was, I didn't do all this work to recover to sit around smoking, eating sweets, feeling crap. I wanted the best drugs whilst using and now I wanted the best recovery feeling! And I really enjoyed feeling good. (But of course it took me a while to get there and the old saying of progress rather than perfection.. The progress was also in the experience of regression to unhealthy habits and back again in cycles until I was totally aware of what worked for me.)

29. Meath's last few thoughts...

It's not about pulling your socks up for someone like me. It's about abstinence through altruism.

Helping others. Not living to serve self.

Finally.

A whole life change. And with that a slow subtle personality change, for the good.

Clean.

All old ideas surrendered.

The only way this worked for me was twelve steps. And not a long drawn-out thing. Just do the motions answer the questions simply, feel the answers, and start again.

And so, help another like you, live for the day, the moment.

And days turn to months, which turn to years and the pain goes away and you laugh again. You can have a spiritual experience of oneness with earth and people and you feel the same as coming up on E's back in the day at times. (If not better.) Or to put it another way whats on offer is the way to a balanced ′normal′ life, free from drugs with peace of mind.

There is much joy to be found and honestly, my best days now have been sober. I got married sober and remember every beautiful minute.

I have had my babies sober and was there, present, to experience the incredible. Thank you, thank you.

Hypnobirthing worked amazingly well and went hand in hand with how I had finally learned to be with my breath... it works even if needing medical intervention. "With my breath I can do anything, I can do anything with my breath." A mantra I use over and over to help calm my mind.

There's hard times, but they aren't half as bad as when the drugs don't work and you want to die for a good fix.

And the best days are true happiness... Not something chemical.

Where am I now?

I am practicing balance. In recovery, home life and pleasure. Without recovery I wouldn't have those things. I have made peace with my demons. No one is perfect. We all make mistakes. I love myself today! (That still feels a little strange to say though.)

When I stop working a programme (which can be very simple and you get into a little routine which barely takes up half an hour a day) and if I start letting ego and materialism take me over, I become negative in my thoughts and towards others. I then see why I used drink and do drugs in the first place. I move into a place of pain, self-obsession and resentful judgement.

I am then thankfully shown my alcoholism by my negative state of mind and how painful it is to feel that way... I remember I am an alcoholic and need to work a programme to be okay with me and therefore others, before I use something. I see how easy it would be to drink in those states of mind and I praise how much the first years of recovery drummed into me my powerlessness over mind-altering substances. Now I can act out with Amazon shopping! But I am aware and I work on it.

I try to live in the moment and enjoy what we have here and now. My life's goal is to live in the present moment, to accept people, places and things just as they are, to not react in a stressed or anxious way to situations real or made up and to not live in fear and worry.

I trust the path I am on is helping me with that. I am not perfect and that is okay. More than okay, it is how

God/source made me. I am finding my life purpose by living this way.

A lot of things that bother me have either already happened or are going to happen in the future. Pointless!
Stopping me from enjoying this precious life today.
When I practice mindfulness and the power of living in the now, all is well. I can't change the past, nor can I control the future. I must live well now!

When I start resenting others, the first place I have to look at is not what they could do better or what they are doing wrong but what I am not doing in my programme and why it is bothering me. Most of the time, if I change my attitude and thinking, my opinion on everyone else changes too.

Am I talking honestly about my feelings with a trusted person? Am I being there for others? Am I helping people and am I connected to and having fun with my new well friends?
If I love myself and am happy then it really doesn't matter. So many things that bother me really aren't that important or relevant in the grand scheme of things.
Everyone is doing the best with what they have and what they are able to give in each moment. I have had to let go of resentments and high expectations. They are a soul killer!
Forgive and forget. Live and love. Be happy, be free. Be. You. And to thine own self be true!

Do things for others. As much as I don't want to, I have to force myself some days to partake in life, to get up and show up and help others, maybe even without telling someone you are doing so! Imagine. No praise from others boosting up my ego! I still struggle with this one!

Helping others is my key to happiness and freedom.

Get out of my head. Literally. I used drugs to get out of my head so now I have to replace that with doing things for others to get out of my head... and it works. I try not to overthink every single thing that occurs! Keeping busy helps that a lot. I decided, after hours of wasted torture with this, that I will be a good person, do good things and try my best. If people don't like that then that is their problem and as long as my side of the street is clean, I am not going to give it another thought. This life is too short to fight everyone's battles.

I know this is easier said than done but the more you practice it the easier it becomes.

Telling the truth and being honest up front when something isn't right and asking for help is also key and really isn't that hard after you have done it a few times. I used to lie about brushing my teeth, where I had been, who I was with, I'd tell you night was day if I could. These things may sound trivial but they all add to the spiritual malady, the unease in the dis-ease and are imperative to a soul change. (Again no pressure, this is after years of practice.)

Meditation for fifteen minutes at morning and night has been a huge help to my peace of mind and learning to get in control of my mind.

I love guided meditations on YouTube, you can also find 12-step ones there. By doing this I also hear messages from my Higher Power, which is amazingly insightful and helpful, especially if I am in a place of pain or moral dilemma.

If we heal ourselves, we will heal the world.

One step at a time.

I would like to thank my mother, Lizbeth, for her unending love, support, help and understanding. Without her dedication to learn about addiction this would have been a

152

much more challenging path. You are one in a million, Ma. I love you to the moon and back.

Even when the path to recovery seems impossible and desperate, keep going, there were so many times I nearly gave up and somehow, I was pulled through by an angel... keep doing the right thing and things will change for the better. And pray, pray, pray! Pray to the sun, to the moon and the stars... Pray to Buddha, Allah, Mary or Jesus... pray to the sea, to the trees and the birds! To the fairies and nature, spirits, whatever you choose! Find out what makes you happy, other than drink and drugs, and go for it! If you can´t face prayer just yet make the meetings and the well people in them your higher power for now and see what evolves.

Keep it simple and don't overthink it all!
x

Taken by Meath; travelling in recovery appreciating natures beauty & finding meetings and recovery friends all over the world.

30. Lizbeth's finale grateful words...

I have learnt so much from my daughter and this hugely difficult experience. I will hold her strength and resolve to live a 'clean' life in my highest esteem.

I will be ever grateful we worked through this with a lot of hard work, tears, stresses, worries, anger and love.

A lot of love held us together over the years, independently through our own pain of anguish, learning, then progress and we are now both in a good place.

I learnt I had very low self-esteem, which was because I went to a boarding school convent at six years old.

I thought if I'd been good enough I wouldn't have been sent away, repeatedly. Then I married a stern, angry man who continually undermined my confidence.

Self-doubt and low confidence was quite natural for much of my life. I have learnt to be aware of this, to not sabotage my current relationships.

For today... we can smile and hope.

When I started writing, I listened to my many voice recordings, how fragile, low, tearful and distraught I sounded.

Then, a year on, it still seemed to sound emotionally exhausted but there were not so many tears.

And finally, these last many months I have the ability to be able to write this, send various chapters to and receive Meath's writings. Both of us growing in our wish to try and explain the hidden knowledge of addiction and how it affects others.

The strongest enlightenment for me was addiction is a disease, an illness, but as it cannot be 'seen' in any other form other than the addict consuming excesses of their drug. Mostly it is viewed to the innocent world as a person that is crazy-looking or needs locking up, or putting away where no one can see them.

I hope these writings may enlighten some of the ignorant critics.

Visible illnesses are treated, accepted as illnesses, allowed financial help on medical insurance policies. Addiction is mostly left out in the cold, seen as unacceptable behaviour and should be swept under the carpet, hidden behind closed doors, not spoken about.

They need and deserve recognition. Help. Understanding. Consideration. Compassion. They have managed within their private meetings. They exist through their own will to self-cure through their meetings. Supporting one another.

I take my hats off to them, they need applause.

I'd like, through these words, for others to see addicts as people, with a mental illness they battle with personally through all of their life.

To see addicts with compassion. If we see someone we may turn our backs on in the street as we are frightened of a drunk or drugged person. I'm not talking about party people, I'm talking about the secret taker. The hidden bag of alcohol drinker, the obsessive house cleaner, the obsessive eater, over- or undereating, and all the other over obsessive-compulsive people, to view them with a kinder more tolerant eye. To send a prayer, to find them help if they ask.

For us to understand more when the obsessive mind can't stop churning, it brings the inability to see things clearly or calmly.

They should not be shunned behind hidden doors, they need our comprehension. Not throwing in prison where they can learn worse behaviours and not be educated and treated for their illness.

Finally, learning how to deal with it all and not allow it to dominate life and move on. Both of us.

I had a wish to help others in similar situations, but it wasn't for me to go to meetings and share my experience in the places Neelam suggested.

Instead, a few years ago I went on a spiritual and meditation path. I read about several different religions.

It was very random reading as I still couldn't concentrate for more than ten or twenty minutes and absorb much. I was trying to learn if there was a reason for all this life of pain, loss, illnesses, traumas.

Soul-searching for answers.

I joined a meditation group where most of the people had suffered many losses and different illnesses in their lives. I felt I belonged there. It suited me somehow. The people were of all different religions including agnostics and spiritualists, it didn't matter.

We all have our own individual way of learning and healing and eventually I found a group I felt at home with and suited me.

I felt relaxed with these private quiet people, searching for some peace and understanding in their life, just as I did.

Several years on and I'm much more confident. I've stopped taking insults and criticism personally. Mentally, I'm much stronger. I have even joined many different art, craft and garden courses.

I don't care so much what people say and don't take it to heart. I still love nature and gardens and I have rescued a few more dogs. There are many interests out in life when one is ready. No rush. I happily go at my pace, not at the speed the world dictates!

The icing on the cake for me will be that writing this will be the clearing out of my painful memories and experiences. Bringing ideas to hopefully help others in similar experiences in their life.

There is hope, there are places and people who can help.

It can be difficult finding people who understand and can help who suit each individual.

Yes, they are there – you just need to find the person and place that is mentally acceptable to you, where you can just listen and talk if you wish and have faith.

Our paths in this life are often so very difficult. To find others who understand is a great help.

Very luckily, I had found someone to teach and advise me.

The alternative for anyone, which I'm sure many people take, is to abandon an addict to a rehab or life on the street. It's your choice, no judgements but none of these bring a real understanding for you and no help for them.

I thought I had lost my precious daughter, to a mind-altering substance which controlled us – yes, us both, because I was immensely affected by it.

Now thankfully it's time to heal and move on.

I've definitely stopped pandering to others, although I still avoid conflict. I'm growing every year in knowledge. I can go out, carry on a conversation! I love life again.

I've stopped crying, at last. What a relief.

I feel our feet are on solid ground now and we're walking the right path.

Most of all, I have my lovely daughter and she is well. We are both independently happy. We are happy when we're together or apart. We are blessed.

As I near the last page, I feel a sudden and real release, I feel it is the right decision to write down for others if they want to read it.

This is the final cleansing. I didn't imagine it would be.

You see, we both had to learn and change – change our way of life, change our friends, only 'you can change you'.

"Grant me the serenity to accept the things I cannot change,
    The courage to change the things I can,
    And the wisdom to know the difference."

Time to heal and move on.

I am not shouting this but I'd like to write this in capitals...

   IT IS NOT THEIR FAULT. IT IS AN ILLNESS.

Thank you, God for my experience and knowledge. .

Forward on... Nil desperandum.

A time to change. Lets wake up to the beauty of the Earth… plant trees, shrubs or flowers for insects, in doing so we ultimately save ourselves. Thrive, connect to source, connect to your breath. See a feather, butterfly, dragonfly… time to transform, HEAL, WAKE UP… Recycle, pick up rubbish. Challenge, question, research, love. Be kind. Open your heart & mind. Meditate. There is much goodness to be found if you set aside your old ideas.

Photo taken in Lizbeths´ magical garden.

CPSIA information can be obtained
at www.ICGtesting.com
Printed in the USA
BVHW031424050819
555095BV00016B/2197/P

9 781789 555547